THE
LIV

Without hesitation I would like to recommend *The Drama of Redemption: Live the Life God Intended.* Dr. Lim is the pastor of a thriving congregation of several thousand in Singapore. I consider him to be one of the finest teachers on gifts of the Holy Spirit in the church world. His understanding of the Charisma gifts, and his clear teaching/writing on related subjects are desperately needed in the body of Christ.

Dr. Wayde Goodall
Pastor and Author

I have known Dr. David Lim for over ten years. His love and passion for Jesus matched only by his biblical scholarship has given him remarkable insight into the beauty and wonder of salvation which makes *The Drama of Redemption: Live the Life God Intended* a must read for anyone who wants to reach the fullness of their potential in Christ.

Ron Johnson
Senior Pastor, Bethel Temple

Exceptional! David Lim lifts the curtain allowing us to observe the importance of each of our lives on this dramatic stage called life. My eyes were opened to Biblical truth, my mind enlightened as to the impact of my daily walk, my heart softened towards those I have relationship with. This is a must read!

Sam Farina
Evangelist

I highly recommend Dr. David Lim's book entitled *The Drama of Redemption: Live the Life God intended* for three primary reasons:

1. **The principles in this book are true and powerful.**
2. **Dr. Lim has lived this message and imparted into my life and countless other people that are destined for God's pleasure.**
3. **Since I have known Dr. Lim for over 25 years, I can assure you that Dr. Lim is living the life God intended for him. He is an inspiration to all of us who have had the pleasure of being in his life.**

Rev. Paul Goulet
Senior Pastor, International Church of Las Vegas

Dr. David Lim, with his great insight into Scripture as a Scholar and Pastor, has written a complementary edition to his book on Spiritual Gifts. It is a book which takes a fresh look at the New Testament Paradigm, that Christians are Actors and Actresses on the Drama of Redemption.

It is a magnificent presentation on redemption, family, spiritual gifts and spiritual warfare that ought to be read and studied by everyone in Pentecostal leadership, and by everyone who wants to live a victorious Christian lifestyle. I look forward to its publication so I can recommend it to our congregation.

Dr. George W. Westlake, Jr.
Senior Pastor (Emeritus)
Sheffield Family Life Center
Kansas City, MO

The Drama *of* Redemption:

Live the Life God Intended

DAVID LIM

OneStoneBooks

THE DRAMA OF REDEMPTION:
LIVE THE LIFE GOD INTENDED

Published by
OneStoneBooks, Singapore
www. onestonebooks.com

Printed and Bound in Malaysia
Cover Design & Interior Design: Ivy Ho

Ordering Information:
Books can be ordered directly from
Grace Assembly of God, Singapore
www.graceaog.org

Or the publisher at
onestonebooks@gmail.com
www.onestonebooks.com

ISBN: 978-981-05-9760-3

My Deepest Appreciation To...

My wife, May, who has been with me and for me every moment of our 37 years together. Truly, without you, there would not be me in the ministry!

Our family, Faith and her husband Brian, Lydia, and Deborah. You have been such an encouragement and strength to me.

The wonderful congregation of Grace Assembly, for whom I first taught the paradigm of the Drama of Redemption. Thanks, too, to a great supportive pastoral and administrative staff, and a strongly united Executive Church Board. I love being your senior pastor.

The graduate students in my class, *Spiritual Gifts: Theology and Practice,* at the Assemblies of God Theological Seminary, who eagerly received this material and urged me to publish it. Sam Farina, Paul Kolbeck, Tim Hogg, and John Carnett took this teaching to another level by publishing *P50, My 50 Day Journey to Empowered Living,* so that churches can put into practice the exercising of spiritual gifts. It is truly a companion volume to this book.

Paul Goulet, who walked me through some really tough times.

George Westlake, the best combination of scholar and visionary pastor that I know.

Ron Johnson, avant garde leader in the apostolic, yet firmly grounded in the Word.

Words cannot express how grateful I am for each of your impartations into my life.

Ivy Ho, publisher of OneStoneBooks, who made this project her own. Your thinking and insight into publishing were invaluable.

Most important, to God be all the glory! If He can use me on the Drama of Redemption, He can use anyone to declare God's victory and Satan's defeat!

David Lim

Contents

CHAPTER 1

THE NEW TESTAMENT PARADIGM

We are actors and actresses in the drama of redemption

Ephesians 3:10; 5:22-25

I believe Ephesians 3:10 is the key to understanding the whole of the book of Ephesians. In this verse Paul leads us to understand a whole new paradigm that would change the way we look at life: our family, our relationships, our job, and, indeed, everything we do. Let's look at what it says:

> "His intent was that now, through the church, the manifold wisdom of God should be made known to the rulers and authorities in the heavenly realms..."

Follow me carefully as I explain the meaning of this verse and other supporting verses. It will revolutionize your life. It did mine. Paul is describing that we are all on the stage of the drama of human redemption. Our audiences are God and His angels on the one hand, and Satan and his demons on the other hand. Pre-believers are watching our lives as well. The saints of ages past are watching. The title of this drama is, "God has won and Satan has lost."

This drama began before the creation of the world when Lucifer mounted a rebellion against God. Who was the devil before he was the devil? He was an angel in heaven. In fact, he led the worship in heaven until one day he tried to exalt himself above God (Isaiah 14:12-15, Ezekiel 28:11-19). God had to judge him and the angels of heaven who followed him in this rebellion (Revelation 12:4, 7, 9). Satan and his demons are watching to see if we will disobey, just like they did. God and His angels are watching us to see if we will obey God's Word.

When we obey God we are declaring the "manifold wisdom of God … to the rulers and authorities in the heavenly realms." We are declaring, when you do it God's way, God wins and Satan loses. We are proclaiming the good news of Jesus Christ to angels as well as to men. We are filling the cosmos with the glory of God.

As a preacher-pastor I used to think I was the actor on the stage and my people were the audience, listening to me preach. Then I began to realize that my preaching was an act of worship to God and that God was my audience. I was not preaching to impress man but God. That was a liberating thought! Now, as I examine Paul's paradigm, I realize that all the powers and authorities of the universe are watching me, to see if I will obey God and therefore declare God's way is the wisest and best way. No matter what I do, if I choose to glorify God, then God wins and Satan loses!

I began to realize that every believer is an actor or actress on the stage of the drama of redemption being watched by God and His angels, the devil and his demons and all those who have not yet believed in Jesus. Our worship, our walk, and our warfare take place on this stage. The drama of the ages is unfolding, and we play vital roles in that drama! Our churches have stages or platforms for the pastor and choir as if they are the key performers. Actually these stages are not biblical, but practical, so that all may see clearly. Biblically, the stage reaches all the way to the back of the church. Every believer is a performer on this stage! And when we leave the church building, the platform moves with us, everywhere we go.

There are other scriptures that bring out this paradigm. In 1 Corinthians 4:9 Paul says,

> "For it seems to me that God has put us apostles on display at the end of the procession, like men condemned to die in the arena. We have been made a spectacle to the whole universe, to angels as well as to men."

The Apostle Paul is saying that the whole universe of angels and men watch our lives! We are put on display. We have become a spectacle!

A similar verse is found in 2 Corinthians 2:14:

> "But thanks be unto God, who always leads us in triumphal procession in Christ and through us spreads everywhere the fragrance of the knowledge of him."

We are marching in a triumphal procession, a parade, and our lives spread the fragrance of the knowledge of Him! In this context the audience is those who are being saved and those who are perishing (2 Corinthians 2:15-16).

Paul confronts the issue of the licentious and liberated women of Corinth. In first century Corinth there were 1,000 priestesses to the goddess Aphrodite, who, as part of their worship, would prostitute themselves on the streets of Corinth by night. They shaved their heads as if to flaunt any rules or expectations of society to submit to authority. This was their advertisement that their bodies were available to men. Paul says:

> "For this reason, and because of the angels, the woman ought to have a sign of authority on her head." (1 Corinthians 11:10)

For many years Bible commentators have had great difficulty with this verse. Did it mean that a woman should wear a veil during church? When I was growing up many women felt it was biblical to wear hats in the service! And, my, what hats they wore! Some looked like they had bouquets of flowers on them, others had fruit on them. As a teenager I wondered why they wore fruit baskets! Also, I was short, so I had difficulty seeing around these ladies to listen to the preacher! The hats became a distraction for my worship! And why does this verse say, "Because of the angels"?

Some interpreters thought that angels could be tempted by the liberated women of Corinth, and therefore the women needed to wear a covering! But the best interpretation is that we are all on the platform of human redemption. Angels, good and evil, are watching our lives. Heaven's angels want us to obey God and submit to His authority. The evil angels, who rebelled against God, want us to disobey God and rebel against God's authority. Paul is telling these liberated women that submission to God's authority is necessary. When we submit we declare that God's way is the best and the wisest way. Thus we declare the rebellious angels have been defeated by Christ on the cross.

We see other evidences of this drama in the book of Job. The title of this scene of the drama is "Will a man serve God for nothing?" Will Job continue to serve God, even if he loses everything? Job 1:6-12 is a scene in heaven where God and Satan are having a discussion. Job is declared by God as upright and blameless. Satan says this is simply because God had blessed Job and protected him. He asks permission to test Job's true obedience. God allows him to do so. Job is not aware of what is happening in the heavenly scene and how involved God and Satan are involved in what shall happen in the following chapters.

In fact, he probably is not even aware that the devil is wrecking havoc upon his life. Old Testament teaching at this point was not very clear on a personal devil. Through all his trials Job does not curse God. He questions, he doubts, he struggles, but he keeps coming to God. He knows his redeemer lives and there will be a judgment after he dies, and he will be declared righteous. Then, in Job 38-42 God speaks clearly to Job first, and then to his friends. God blesses Job more greatly in his latter days than the former days. Job is justified before his wife, his friends, all his neighbors, and even the devil.

Even a brief study of the role of angels throughout the Bible reveals their vital involvement in the drama of redemption. An angel guards the way to the tree of life in the Garden of Eden (Genesis 3:24). Angels tell Abraham that he shall have a son (Genesis 18). Isaac will be the child of promise through whom the Messiah would come. An angel wrestles with Jacob the deceiver and changes him to Israel, one who has struggled with God and with men and has overcome. An angel commissions Joshua to take Jericho (Joshua 5:13-15). An angel challenges Gideon to deliver Israel (Judges 6). A demonic force, the prince of Persia hindered Daniel's prayers for 21 days, but Michael the archangel came to help overcome the resistance.

Then we come to Jesus' life and ministry on earth. Will Jesus obey the Father's will? Or will He shrink from the great task of redemption for mankind? Satan comes to tempt Him (Matthew 4:1-13, Luke 4:1-13). Over the years many scholars have debated the question, could Jesus have sinned? Actually that is not even the issue of the three temptations. The three temptations are actually messianic temptations. What kind of Messiah would Jesus be?

What role would He play? Would He be the Messiah of His Father's expectations, or would He be the Messiah of man's expectations?

Jesus would not have sinned by turning the stones to bread. In fact, later He turns five loaves and two fishes into enough food to feed five thousand men, besides women and children. But He would not use His power for His own purpose, to exalt Himself.

The Jewish people were expecting an earthly political Messiah, who would provide a banquet in the wilderness. Jesus said to Satan, "Man does not live on bread alone" (Luke 4:4). Then the devil showed Him all the kingdoms of the world in an instant, offering to give everything to Jesus. He was tempting Jesus to not face the cross and still be the King over the world. He could be an earthly king. Jesus replied, "Worship the Lord your God, and serve Him only."

On the third temptation, Satan leads Jesus to the pinnacle of the temple and challenges Him to jump off and the angels would rescue Him! If the huge crowds below saw Him jump and not die, they would have instantly crowned Him as their Messiah. Jesus says, "Do not put the Lord your God to the test." Simply put, Jesus obeyed His Father's plan and purpose. He would suffer for all of mankind. He would vanquish the devil. When Jesus died on the cross, He declared, "It is finished" (John 19:30 can also be translated, "it has been accomplished"). In this triumphal act of redemption, Jesus declared that God has won and Satan has lost.

Hebrews 12:1 says, "We are surrounded by such a great cloud of witnesses" referring to all the saints of the Old Testament and all those believers who have gone on before us. They are cheering us on. They are watching our lives. They want their lives to be an inspiration to us, so we may run the race well. Further development of this paradigm of the drama of redemption is found in the book of Revelation.

The whole book represents a drama of salvation history. The angels and the redeemed of all ages are singing songs of the glory and victory of God. In the book of Revelation we see that the angels are vitally involved in unfolding the plan of God on behalf of the redeemed saints. Even the prayers of all the saints are kept in a vial, ready to be poured out in judgment upon evil.

Satan and his evil colleagues are doing all they can to destroy the works of God and the people of God. But God has a plan. In Revelation 20 we see that God binds Satan for a thousand years, while the saints rule and reign upon the earth.

This reign for one thousand years will reveal what can happen when we truly submit to God. Paul referred to this day in 1 Corinthians 6:2-3, "Do you not know that the saints will judge the world? … Do you not know that we will judge angels?"

Then, there is a final battle, the battle of Gog and Magog, where Satan is finally defeated and cast into the lake of fire and tormented day and night forever. At that point (Revelation 20:11), we see the Great White Throne Judgment. This is where all peoples are judged according to what they have done. This will be the time that every knee shall bow before Jesus and every tongue will confess that Jesus is Lord. All who disobeyed and rebelled against God will be summarily judged.

It is not that they have not already been judged, but Revelation pictures this as the culminating act to the drama of redemption. Those whose names are found in the Book of Life will not face the second death. Those who are not found in the Book of Life will face eternal judgment. The drama of human redemption comes to a dramatic climax as God creates the new heavens and the new earth, and the New Jerusalem comes down from heaven (Revelation 21).

This paradigm puts together the cosmic perspective of redemption, spiritual warfare, spiritual gifts, and powerful lifestyles that glorify God, touch man, and defeat the devil.

In *Section One*, I will share the practical implications of how this New Testament paradigm works out in the family. Dynamic, biblical marriage is actually a declaration of how Christ loves the church and how the church submits to Christ. This is the truth that defeats the devil! Everything we do in this drama becomes an act of worship to God! I shall even document how sex in marriage is an act of worship!

This paradigm revolutionizes our perspective of family and parent-child relationships. When parents and children play out their role properly, their unity will destroy Satan's craftiness and attack on the family. Parents will empower their children, and children will empower their parents! Singles, too, play a huge role in this drama. They can be focused and fulfilled soldiers in God's army!

Section Two will focus on the church in the drama. When we see the New Testament picture of the church we will see our corporate role in this drama. The church is God's instrument to declare God's glory throughout the cosmos! The script for the drama is found in the five New Testament words for ministry: worship, fellowship, proclamation, teaching, and service. We will see worship as a lifestyle and how worship empowers our lifestyle through the baptism of the Holy Spirit. Because we are the prophetic people of God, we will learn practical principles of ministering spiritual gifts. Spiritual gifts are God's tools for us to play our vital role in the drama. We will learn that when we know our role, the gifts will flow.

In *Section Three*, I will discuss how to touch our world and fill the universe with the glory of God (Ephesians 1:22-23). The platform of the drama moves wherever we go. We see our special mission and holy calling to the marketplace, where we work. Integrity is the key character strength we must have to face every challenge in the drama. Finally, I will conclude with a survey of Ephesians 1-6 to see an overview of the drama and how it incorporates the worship, walk, and warfare of the saints. When we live out the principles of this drama, our lives will be more fulfilled and satisfying than ever! We will confidently face every challenge and conquer all confusion! More importantly, we shall live the lives God intended, and shall change our world!

PART 1

The Family

The family structure is under attack worldwide. Satan is the great enemy of marriages. Broken marriages lead to spiritual and emotional bondages. We can defeat the devil here! I believe one of the greatest testimonies for the Christian church shall be strong families. Malachi 4:6 talks about an Elijah ministry in the last days: "He will turn the hearts of the fathers to their children, and the hearts of the children to their father; or else I will come and strike the land with a curse."

We need a whole new paradigm about how to see families. Families offer covering, protection from attack, self esteem, strength and the keys to unlocking the authority structure of the universe! Chapter Two puts marriage in the biblical context of enabling one another for ministry! Chapter Three reveals sex on the highest plane, rarely taught, nor understood, nor practiced. Chapter Four changes our concepts of parenting. Our task is to represent Father God! Further, children have a responsibility to minister to their parents! Chapter Five exalts the single life that is totally dedicated to God's glory.

CHAPTER 2

BIBLICAL MARRIAGE DEFEATS THE DEVIL!

Marriage Is to Enable Your Spouse for Ministry, and that Ministry Defeats Satan!

Let us see how this paradigm of the drama of redemption applies in our daily context. In Ephesians 5:21-27 Paul says:

> "Submit to one another out of reverence for Christ.
>
> Wives, submit to your husbands as to the Lord. For the husband is the head of the wife as Christ is the head of the church, his body, of which he is the Savior. Now as the church submits to Christ, so also wives should submit to their husbands in everything.
>
> Husbands, love your wives, just as Christ loved the church and gave himself up for her to make her holy, cleansing her by the washing with water through the word, and to present her to himself as a radiant church, without stain or wrinkle or any other blemish, but holy and blameless."

There are two ways to interpret this passage of scripture. Traditionally we have preached that how Christ loved the church models how husbands are to love their wives. Further, how the church submits to Christ is the model of how wives are to submit to their husbands. I have nothing against this interpretation. I have preached it! The only problem is that the wife says, "When my husband loves me as Christ loves the church, then I will submit to him." The husband says, "I just wish my wife would submit to me! Then I could love her like Christ loved the church!" So rather than a solution, we have a greater problem!

No husband is perfect like Christ. None of us can love as completely as Christ loves. No wife can find her submission perfect either. It is so much easier to submit to the Lord than to her husband!

The second way to interpret this passage of scripture is in the context of the drama of human redemption. Angels, good and rebellious, are watching us. When I love my wife I declare to the heavenly angels and the demonic forces that this is how Christ loved the church! I am preaching the gospel to the principalities and powers of the cosmos and to the pre-believers. When I love my wife God's way, then God wins and Satan loses! I am telling Satan to get lost because I will cover my wife with the love of God. But too many men put a full stop, a period after "husbands, love your wives ..." And they say, "But I love my wife with all my heart!" That is not what this passage says. This command to love our wives goes much further. We are to love our wives, to make her holy, to set her apart for fulfillment in God's ministry for her life! My calling as a husband is to develop my wife to her fullest potential for God! It goes further yet!

In this drama of redemption, marriage is to make you holy, not just to make you happy. Ephesians 5:25-32 tells husbands to do several things:

1. "Love your wives..." (Ephesians 5:25). This proclaims to angels and principalities and pre-believers that this is how Christ loves the church.

2. "Give yourself up for her..." (Ephesians 5:25). Model Christ's redemptive love for all to see. It is sacrificial, unconditional, godly love.

3. "Make her holy..." (Ephesians 5:26). Holy means set apart for ministry. Therefore, the husband's role is to develop the wife's ministry. He must fulfill her potential as a woman of God. His is vision–oriented leadership. His calling, as God's appointed leader, is to build her spiritually, emotionally, esteem-wise, and ministry-wise to be all she can be! How many husbands have thought of marriage in this way?

4. "Cleansing her by the washing of water through the word" (Ephesians 5:26). Husbands are to cleanse their wives by the washing with water through the "word." "Word" is ***rhema***, referring to the spoken word. Men are to speak words of love, forgiveness and affirmation, just like Jesus. Women are more verbal, while men are more visual. Research has shown the average woman speaks twice as many words per day as the average man.

   As a woman she needs words of kindness and affection. That builds her spirit and her inner beauty. That brings forgiveness and grace into her life.

   When Adam and Eve sinned, Adam first blamed Eve and Eve then blamed the serpent. But Adam spoke words of hope and blessing, cleansing and redemption, when he named his wife Eve. He said she would be the mother of all living (Genesis 3:20). Instead of saying she was the heart of his problems and the cause of sin in the world, he spoke of her as one to be respected as the mother of the human race! She was esteemed in his sight. Any wife would be blessed by her husband if he kept speaking blessing into her life!

5. "And present her to himself as a radiant church..." (Ephesians 5:27). Bring out all her God given glory, beauty, talent, ministry and joy! The husband's goal is not just a peaceful, happy marriage and personal fulfilment. His goal is to develop his wife into a joyful, radiant, woman of God!

   Marriage is not to make you happy, but to make you holy (set apart for God's purposes)! Husbands stand in Christ's stead, to present their wives to Christ as the church in all her glory! As a pastor, I have a huge responsibility to develop Grace Assembly to her full potential, to glorify God in every way possible. That same responsibility is the husband's in relationship to his wife.

6. Three times God commands husbands in this passage to love your wives! (Ephesians 5:22, 28, 33). We are to continue to romance our wives for the entire marriage! We are to lavish love on her! This is not an option. It is a command!

7. "He who loves his wife loves himself. After all, no one ever hated his own body, but he feeds and cares for it, just as Christ does the church..." (Ephesians 5:28-29). In loving your wife you love yourself and do yourself a great favor. She blossoms. She blesses her husband.

8. "For this reason a man will leave his father and mother and be united to his wife, and the two will become one flesh" (Ephesians 5:31-32). In loving our wives this way, the two become one. In so doing we are declaring the profound mystery of the

> relationship of Christ and the church. The wife is to submit to her husband as to the Lord. "Submit" has become a negative word in our world. Pictures of a demanding, unreasonable, and harsh husband telling the poor defeated wife what to do are the first thoughts in many people's minds.

Many husbands miss the point entirely. They take the "cave man approach." They think they must force their wives into submission. Or, give a command and expect it to be followed. Then they are frustrated when that does not happen. They feel like failures.

Leadership is never this simplistic. It always involves investment of time, caring, planning, strategizing, communication, shared goals, integrity of character and purpose. Why is it that we as men know what we must do to lead in the workplace and yet do not apply these same principles at home?

There is abuse going on in some homes. That must not be tolerated. But biblical submission is not suppression! Submission is to do those things that the Lord would want us to do. It is not a blind submission that says "yes, sir!" regardless of the request. Biblical submission follows Jesus' example, who willingly submitted to the Father's will. It is the full sharing of all that we are to lift the marriage to an even higher level.

Submission must be taken in the full biblical context. "So God created man (Hebrew: mankind) in his own image, in the image of God He created him, male and female he created them (Genesis 1:27)." He gave them dominion over the face of the earth (Genesis 1:27-30). This meant both male and female are made in the image of God and are to be deeply respected as co-rulers over the earth. Male and female were created as equals in the sight of God. Only mankind (male and female) was created in the image of God. Great dignity belongs to every human being. There must be mutual respect for God's calling on the man and the woman.

Women are not only to be co-rulers with men over the creation, they have holy callings for God given ministries. We are all priests unto God. That means both husband and wife are priests. Just as the husband provides a spiritual covering for the wife, the wife is a covering for the husband. I seek to protect my wife against spiritual attack. She is able to do the same for me. When I operate under her covering and delight, the whole congregation knows how strong our marriage is. They trust my integrity, motives and actions.

When we are in agreement on the key issues, we become a powerful spiritual force. In a single parent family, the woman often has to function as the head of the household. This is her Christian role and duty. And many have been mightily blessed of God in fulfilling this role.

Since the Holy Spirit was poured out upon all flesh on the Day of Pentecost, a prophetic anointing comes upon women as well as men. Philip's daughters were prophetesses. Priscilla was likely the more prominent spiritual leader in the home of Aquila and Priscilla. Even Junia (Romans 16:7) was known as an apostle. All the spiritual gifts may be ministered through women as well as men. Women are not limited in their scope of ministry in the New Testament. They play priestly and prophetic roles.

Submission is in the context of mutual submission. Ephesians 5:21 says,"Submit to one another out of reverence for Christ." In the body of Christ we must also share the servant spirit of our Lord. We seek to build each other up. We seek to be Christlike towards one another. Jesus' submission to the Father was not a blind submission. He willingly submitted all that He had to do the Father's will.

When students submit research papers to the professor they are to share all their study, insight and opinion in such a way that the professor receives it gladly. The wife has an obligation before God to share her insights and perspectives to help her husband make the best decision possible. She needs to share it in a way that her husband can receive it well. She does not seek to domineer or lord it over her husband. But she realizes he cannot make the decision alone. He needs input. As the wife submits to her husband, it is not that she trusts him to make the right decision at every point. It takes a very secure woman to submit all that she is.

Rather, she trusts the sovereign God who watches over her life to take care of her. I've made a lot of mistakes, financially and otherwise, in our marriage! But my wife knows she is safely in the hands of Heavenly Father. When she submits her ideas, opinions, feelings in the proper manner, she declares to the rebellious angels, that when you do it God's way, God wins and Satan loses! Then Satan has to flee from our families. Then husband and wife can offer a covering for each other and for their family.

When "wives submit to their husbands as to the Lord", the wife develops his headship or leadership (Ephesians 5:22-23). One of man's key needs from his wife is admiration and respect. A man can endure much criticism from outside the family, but a constant negative word from the wife can destroy his will and motivation.

A godly woman wants her husband's headship. He is her covering. He is high priest in the home. She wants him to develop his ministries so he can bless the family, the church, and the society. So submission is actually a strategy to draw out the best in him! It is not from a position of inferiority. Someone has to make the final decision and bear the final responsibility. God appointed the husband to this role. (In a single-parent family the single parent whether man or woman becomes the final authority.)

This in turn becomes a great witness to the husband. Peter says, that unsaved husbands can be won to the Lord without words through the "purity and reverence of your lives", through "the unfading beauty of a gentle and quiet spirit", through wives who "do what is right and do not give way to fear" (1 Peter 3:1-6).

Peter pictures a wife who has her trust and confidence in God. That is why she does not lose control. Submission declares God is in control, not Satan. Submission is a strategy to draw out the leadership skills of the husband, to help him learn to bear responsibility and to receive adequate input. It allows him to grow, and even to make mistakes.

I remember a young married couple who were my students when I taught Bible college in Canada. She was a very talented pastor's daughter. She could preach, teach, play piano and sing. She married a shy, reserved, insecure carpenter who felt a call to the ministry. He felt intimidated by her, to say the least. But she developed a strategy. While still serving the Lord wholeheartedly, she began to develop his gifts and strengths. She lifted him up as the leader of the home. Later they went as missionaries to Africa. He became the senior pastor of a very large church.

When I met them at a school of missions in Canada, he had grown in self confidence and ability. God was using him mightily. As we shared concerning how far God had brought him, she wept freely and joyfully. Indeed, God had answered her prayers and made him a leader! The purpose of the wife's submission is threefold:

1. To declare that God's way is the best way and to declare to the rebellious angels that they were wrong in rebelling. Submission is really a prophetic act.

2. The submission is really to the Lord. We trust that God watches over us!

3. To develop the husband's leadership and ministry gifts.

These instructions given to husband and wife are in the form of commands that an officer of the army gives a soldier. They are not simply cute suggestions and hoped for results. God gives the commands to the husband unilaterally, whether or not she submits. God tells the wife to submit as to the Lord, whether or not the husband's love is as unselfish or perfect as Christ's love. We are in a spiritual warfare and the enemy seeks to do all he can to destroy marriages and families.

In America the divorce rate is at about 50%. In Korea it has reached 47%, in Hong Kong 41%, in Japan 38%. Singapore has jumped from a 15% divorce rate in 1990 to 26% in 2002 (*Time Research* 16 April 2004). With the rapid increase in urbanization, growth in technology, and pressures of globalization, families must confront higher expectation levels and stress. When we see our lives in the drama of human redemption we learn to fight the right battles and use the right methodology.

I shall discuss the chart below, but first look at the following contrasts: The left column describes the biblical approach. The right column describes the sad reality in many marriages.

1. Spiritual Warfare: defeat Satan.	Wrong battles: fight family.
2. Fulfill potential of spouse through grace and forgiveness.	Frustrated by unfulfilled expectations.
3. Understand God's Power Structure: Love and submit through mutual submission.	Fight over money, sex, and communication.

4. Unconditional, sacrificial love.	Love must be earned.
5. Parents offer a covering for the family.	Generational curses affect the family.
6. The family is seen as the key to touch the world for Christ.	The family is seen as the obstacle to our personal ambitions.
7. We must submit to God's commands.	Submit to selfish desires.

1. **Biblically we know that the greatest enemy of all that is good and right in our families is Satan himself.** I have often said our enemy is not the spouse, the children, or the in-laws. It is Satan. We expend far too much energy and emotion to win fights and arguments in our families. We see other members of the family as our enemies. But in the drama of redemption we realize we have a holy calling to minister to our families. The husband must offer unconditional love to his wife. The wife must seek to minister to her husband's needs. Together, they seek to impart spiritual life into their children. As they do so, Satan is defeated and God is exalted.

2. **Christ loved us in order to set us apart for service to God and fulfill His purpose in creating us.** When we speak words of grace and forgiveness instead of criticism and harshness, we help each other to fulfill our potential in Christ. Our lives are to be a song of thanksgiving to Christ. We do what we do, not because we have to, but because we are so grateful! In fact, I

do not deserve anything from God at all. I do not deserve my wife. She is God's gift to me. I do not expect anything from her. Yet every little thing she does for me is a gift of grace. When she cooks a meal, or takes care of the laundry, I feel I am so privileged. I do not deserve that, yet she lovingly does all that for me! Of course, that works both ways. I am God's gift of grace to her. She does not make demands on me, but loves me unconditionally. She appreciates the little things I do for her.

The very opposite takes place in most marriages. The biggest issue of marriages in our day is unfulfilled expectations. It seems the more material possessions we get, the more knowledge we have, the more lifestyle conveniences we have, the higher our expectations of one another. Marriage counselors have discovered that understanding communication techniques alone is not the solution to marriage problems. Many use communication skills to hurt one another instead of to help one another. Even communications experts have found their families falling apart. Spouses become more demanding and less flexible. Marriage for a lifetime is not seen as a treasured holy value.

We should see our role as giving, rather than receiving, of freeing the potential of our spouses rather than making demands of them.

3. **God has a power structure that truly empowers families.** When families learn how to submit to that structure everyone is blessed. The first principle is found in Ephesians 5:21. Mutual submission is the umbrella for this power structure. We are to submit to one another out of reverence for Christ. We do it for Christ's sake. It is not lording over our spouse or nagging the spouse until he/she does something. We must understand that we are part of the body of Christ, and as members, we are interdependent. Underlying the wife's submission is

mutual submission as members of Christ's body. Submission is a beautiful word. A runner submits his mind and body to rigorous discipline so that he may win the race. A medical student submits himself to the heavy load of studies so he can become the best doctor possible. A musician disciplines himself to practice until the music flows forth from him. And, as actors and actresses on the drama of redemption, we submit our best service to God so that we can declare by our lives that God has won and Satan has lost.

Why are so many families powerless, divided, and struggling? Husbands and wives fight over money, sex, and communication. They are in a battle between the sexes. They try to gain the upper hand as if to say "I win, you lose." There is no strong example set for the children. We inadvertently give place to the devil. To these couples, Paul would say, "Submit yourselves to one another, out of reverence for Christ" (Ephesians 5:21). Submit for Jesus' sake!

4. **Jesus showed us sacrificial, unconditional love.** I have heard men say, "If my wife would change in these three ways, then things would be all right." I have heard women say, "He is the one who must do the changing." Human love is based on earning that love. We learn this from the time we are children. "If you will do these things then mommy and daddy will love you. If not, we will not love you anymore!" I heard my mother say when I was a child "Mommy loves a good boy. If you are naughty, the gorillas will eat you up!" Because we have high expectations for others we expect them to live up to our expectations. "She's my wife. Of course she should do those things.""He's my husband. He should understand me better than that!"

Rather, Jesus showed us divine love (*agape* in Greek). The greatest example of divine love was the cross of Calvary. His love was full of purpose: to redeem us and forgive us. It was sacrificial: He gave His all. It was unconditional: whether or not we loved Him in return, He unilaterally gave His life for us! It is this kind of love that builds solidity, fulfillment and excitement in a marriage. Even in the act of intimacy in marriage, Paul's key to sexual fulfillment is that we seek to fulfill the spouse's needs.

When both husband and wife seek to fulfill each other, then both are most fulfilled (1 Corinthians 7:3-5). It is hard for us to accept the fact that God loves us unconditionally because so much of this world's love is conditional. But God says "I love you simply because I love you." Keep showing this kind of love and you will chase the devil out of your marriage!

5. **Parents offer a covering for the family.** God created the family unit. It is meant to be powerful. But it can only be powerful if parents provide a covering for the family. Every morning I pray this prayer over my wife and for my children: "I cover you with the love of Jesus and the blood of Jesus. I am the spiritual gateway to the family. No enemy can attack unless he comes through me first, and I reject the attack of the enemy." Then my wife covers us with the armor of God.

   This way I assume my responsibility as the head of the house. I protect the family from enemy attack. Of course, that means I also shall not be the one to attack my family! Just as I cover my wife and family, my wife covers us as parents.

   As long as we are in unity and our marriage is strong, we provide a covering of protection for our children. When our children stay under that covering they are protected from the devil's attacks. On the other hand, if our marriage is full of conflict, it leaves holes in the covering of protection for our children. If there is a divorce or abuse, generational curses come upon the children and future generations. Studies have shown that the key cause of poverty in America today is broken families! Children from divorced families have a greater possibility of divorce themselves.

Counselors indicate that many emotional and personality problems stem from the lack of parental warmth, especially from the father. Most prisoners would say they hate their father, or at the least, have no warm feelings for their father. Years ago, I led a class for abused wives in Canada. What shocked me was there were three mothers there whose daughters were there as well! The mothers had married abusive husbands and the daughters had done the same! Only the grace of God can stop this vicious cycle of generational curses.

6. **The family is seen as the key to touching the world for Christ.** I believe with all my heart that the miracle in the last days that will really touch the world is that of a solid Christian family. Of course I believe in signs and wonders and miracles. But we are seeing such a breakdown of the family worldwide that I believe this is one of Satan's strategies to cause chaos to reign.

   The Christian family will stand dramatically against the wiles of the devil. Biblically, the husband's role is to develop the wife for her ministry. The wife's role is to strategize on how to lift her husband's leadership role. The parents' role is to represent Father God to their children: to share unconditional love and holiness, to disciple them in the image of Christ, to reveal God's grace, and to empower them to fulfill God's plan for their lives. They are not to "exasperate their children; instead bring them up in the training and instruction of the Lord" (Ephesians 6:4).

   Instead, I've heard, "my greatest hindrance to serving God is my family". "If only my wife will submit to me, then we could really serve the Lord" or "my husband will not take his role as the spiritual leader". Begin to see your spouse as God sees him/her. Use the God-ordained strategies of love and submission to develop your spouse to full potential. Pray. Minister in Jerusalem before you think of the ends of the earth.

7. **We must submit to God's commands.** The commands of Ephesians 5 are military commands. They are those of a captain ordering a private on what to do. We are in spiritual warfare. If we are going to win this battle we need to unite to fight the enemy. Ultimately our submission is first to God, then to one another.

   If we are fully submitted to God we will obey His command to submit to one another. We will do things God's way. We will not act out of emotion, reaction, or revenge. We will seek the best for one another, because in our families we are doing the work of God and we are defeating Satan. Many times this truth has helped me. I may be tempted to make the wrong decision or say something hurtful to the family, but I choose not to, because in this drama of redemption, I declare by my actions and words, "God wins and Satan loses."

Looking at life through the paradigm of the drama of redemption changes our whole perspective. With a changed perspective comes changed actions, words and purposes. And this applies in every area of our lives: marriage, parenting, employer-employee relationships, friendships, business practices—everything. You are an actor or actress in this great drama—and a richly rewarded one, I might add! You will inherit eternal life. You will walk on streets of gold. You will reign with Christ! Play your part well. You are showing the wisdom of God to all the principalities and powers in the heavenly realm. You are affecting the whole cosmos for eternity's sake!

Happiness is never to be an end in itself, but a by-product of a right relationship with God and a right paradigm on life. This is the opposite view of those who expect to be fulfilled in the marriage. Yet, when you see that marriage is to make you holy, not to primarily make you happy, the amazing result is that you will find great happiness and joy in marriage! If you marry hoping that he/she will fulfill your needs and make you happy you will be frustrated. However, if you marry someone with whom you may share commitment, love and growth in Christ, then happiness comes in great measure. Seek to glorify God.

The Christian marriage follows a different paradigm:

- Rather than living by fear, we live by faith in God.

- Rather than seeking happiness as our goal in marriage, we allow marriage to make us holy.

- Rather than finding the right one, I need to be the right one

- Rather than relying on communication skills alone, we also seek to build trust, show unconditional love, and create a safe haven for our spouse.

- Rather than insisting that our wives obey us, we do our part first by loving our wives as Christ loved the church. We seek to develop their full potential.

- Rather than sharing limited, conditional love, we share God's unconditional love.

- Rather than refusing to submit to husbands, wives need to think of creative ways to lift husbands to a higher level of leadership so they can bless the family more.

- Rather than living out our marriage in the humdrum of earthly existence, we need to see the larger picture. We seek to be a witness for the glory of God.

CHAPTER 3

SEX AS AN ACT OF WORSHIP

Go One Level Higher in Sexual Fulfillment!

Genesis 2:22-25; 3:20; 4:1

The sexual area of life has been hushed up by well-meaning Christians for too long. I have tried to lay out the argumentation of sex as an act of worship carefully and concisely for you in this chapter. I pray it will clarify the profundity of the sexual relationship and why it belongs exclusively within marriage.

Some singles, without much thought, wish for the intimacy of a sexual relationship without the accompanying responsibility of marriage. That only brings pain in relationships, a selfish manipulating of the other person for one's gratification, and a higher rate of divorce. The Bible has clearly built walls around marriage to protect the sacredness of the marital relationship. Marriage is difficult enough without tearing down those walls.

When those walls are broken down through premarital or extramarital sex, the spiritual-emotional covering of protection is no longer there. And the demons will use that to attack moral values and our marriages. Trust is then broken down, pain is inflicted, and forgiveness and the rebuilding of the relationship takes much hard work over a long period of time.

It is important to know the unique place of sex within the marital relationship to begin to understand why the Bible speaks so strongly against fornication and adultery.

Study the book of Proverbs and you will see why "stolen water is sweet; food eaten in secret is delicious! But little do they know that the dead are there, that her guests are in the depths of the grave" (Proverbs 9:17-18).

We have young people who don't know how to cope with their inner drives and emotions. We have married couples who downplay the need for fulfillment in this area or are too busy to minister to their spouse's needs, and thus do not have their own needs met.

My prayer is that singles will understand the sanctity of sex in marriage; and married couples will not take this area for granted but minister to each other's lives through it. Singles can read my chapter on being a focused and fulfilled single to learn how to handle their sexual drive prior to marriage better.

I will lay out a chart before you and then explain each point further. From the Biblical perspective, sex:

IN MARRIAGE	OUTSIDE OF MARRIAGE
1. Intimate knowing: spirit, soul, and body. Crowns marriage relationship. One flesh (Gen. 2:24, Eph. 5:31).	1. Shortcuts true knowing. Refuses to pay price for commitment, relationship, and communication. Focuses on initiation of relationship rather than fulfilling climax.
2. Intimacy, not shame (Gen. 2:23-25).	2. Condemnation, guilt, shame.
3. Redemptive, healing (Gen. 4:1).	3. Destructive, unfulfilling in long term.
4. Celebration of God's grace-worship (1 Cor. 6:19-20 body is temple).	4. Demonic bondage (1 Cor. 6:15).
5. Built on covenant and commitment (1 Cor 7:3-5).	5. Built on vain wishes. Breaks covenant.
6. Expresses grace (1 Cor. 7:3-5).	6. Earned love—if you meet my expectations.
7. Enjoyment grows.	7. Enjoyment declines.
8. Guards against temptations (1 Cor. 7:5).	8. Falls into Satan's trap (1 Cor. 7:2).

IN MARRIAGE	OUTSIDE OF MARRIAGE
9. Frees couple to serve God (1 Cor. 7:9).	9. Compromises effective service.
10. Covering for family (1 Cor. 7:14).	10. No covering, no trust, no long-term commitment.
11. One flesh parallels Christ's relationship to the church (Eph. 5:32).	11. Sex is Lust.
12. Eros redeemed by Agape.	12. Eros Defiled.

1. INTIMATE KNOWING

In Genesis 4:1, the NIV simply translates "Adam lay with his wife". The KJV says "Adam knew his wife". The actual idea behind the original Hebrew is a full knowing of the person. The sexual relationship is meant to crown a relationship built upon full knowledge of the person. This means thorough communication, genuine communion, and total commitment.

The phrase "one flesh" meant far more than just the physical in biblical times. Flesh or body represented the whole person–body, soul, and spirit. The consummation of a union between male and female is thus characterized as a union to become one flesh. It takes time and the safety of total commitment to truly enjoy the sexual relationship without shame or fear of tragic betrayal. We all want intimate relationships and the sexual relationship is meant to crown the intimacy that comes with total commitment to one another in marriage.

Yet too often people want a shortcut to intimacy. They focus only on the physical aspects of intimacy, thinking those feelings represent the real thing. Their focus is on the initiation of the relationship rather than the full "knowing" of the other person. That is why people on single dates begin physical intimacy too early. They tend not to know what to talk about or what to do, so they begin experimenting with the physical side of a relationship. Then they lose control and go too far. This inevitably breaks down trust. If a person can make love to me outside of marriage, who else will he/she make love to?

People who have one sexual partner outside of marriage will likely have several sexual partners in their lifetime. After disagreements, they think all they have to do is "kiss and make up." This rarely solves the problems. The real problems that must be carefully confronted are overlooked.

2. BUILDS INTIMACY, NOT SHAME

Genesis 2:23-25 contains powerful concepts of marriage which form the basis of much of Paul's teaching on marriage.

The wife is to be an integral part of the man—bone of his bone, flesh of his flesh. Eve came from Adam. There is an intimate unity, spiritually, emotionally and physically. This kind of relationship can only come with proper walls of protection and commitment. It takes a lot of work. There is a psychological and emotional leaving behind of the parental covering to form a new covering. They join in a process of becoming one flesh (Genesis 2:24). The one flesh relationship indicates how close a man and wife should be and how they are to stand in agreement on the major issues.

There was no shame in this relationship (Genesis 2:25). The sexual relationship in marriage is not evil. It is pure, holy, and wonderful. But Satan has made sex to be filthy, selfish, and dishonoring to God, something only people with evil minds talk about. Even Christian couples have a difficult time talking about this area of their marriage. I am amazed at how many couples have dysfunctional relationships sexually. Yet God created sex! It pictures the one flesh relationship. It seals the marriage covenant.

Hebrews 13:4 says, "Marriage should be honored by all, and the marriage bed kept pure, for God will judge the adulterer and all the sexually immoral." Outside of marriage, sex becomes a mere act of physical intimacy alone, accompanied by spiritual bondage. We shall discuss the bondage part later. It will ultimately bring a sense of condemnation and guilt because it violates the sacredness of marriage and breaks down walls of trust.

This shame was apparent in Genesis 3:10-11 when Adam and Eve hid in the Garden of Eden and they were naked. In the purity of the husband-wife relationship they were not ashamed. When sin entered the picture, all was thrown out of perspective. Sex outside of marriage leaves nothing sacred in marriage. The deepest, most intimate relationship of marriage is no longer protected.

3. Redemptive healing

One can scarcely imagine the complete devastation of Adam and Eve's sin. Adam blamed Eve, Eve blamed the serpent. God had to judge sin. This sin caused Adam and Eve to be cast out of the Garden of Eden. They would have to work hard to till the land. There would be pain in childbirth. Their children would take on a sinful nature. Their sin would affect all mankind. All mankind would suffer from having a sinful nature and living in a sinful world. In the midst of this judgment God promised that from the woman would come redemption that would crush Satan's head (Genesis 3:15). Instead of simply judging Eve, God said that man's hope would come through her! This was a prophecy that the Messiah would come from woman and ultimately defeat Satan! The Messiah would redeem mankind from sin and give us hope.

After this judgment from God, Adam began to take his responsibility as the head of the home. He believed God's promise that Eve's offspring would crush the serpent's head. Instead of blaming her he called his wife Eve–the mother of all living (Genesis 3:20).

I would have been tempted to name her "Awful" instead of Eve! What she had done would affect all mankind! And man has been blaming woman for his problems since then! Instead, Adam became a spiritual covering for her. He took the ultimate responsibility. Instead of blaming Eve, Adam spoke graciously to her and honored her. He made love to her and they had children (Genesis 4:1-2).

Eve rejoiced that her husband loved her and that God had helped her bring forth children. Biblically, the Redeemer would come through birth as a human being. Adam's love brought healing to Eve's spirit—she knew she was loved and forgiven. To this day, sex in marriage renews the human spirit. It lifts couples up from the pain and hurts the world may inflict upon them because they know they have each other and seek to build up each other. Within marriage, sex is re-**creation**-al. It gives the couple energy, healing, and hope to move ahead in life.

Sex outside of marriage is none of these beautiful things. Outside of marriage, one may just view sex as "recreational". One dear member of our church told me that outside of marriage it should be spelt "wreck-reational"! It may seem thrilling for a moment or even for a period of time, but ultimately it is destructive, because there is no permanence in the relationship. It cannot be a lasting fulfillment because sex should be within the boundaries of true, unconditional, and permanent commitment. The *Straits Times* reported that out of one hundred and four delinquent teenagers under sixteen years of age, thirty three already had sex and ten have had multiple sex partners. One girl, aged fourteen, had already slept with forty-seven men! A January 2005 survey in the *Sunday Times* revealed that four in ten teens thought premarital sex was acceptable! In a survey conducted at the National University of Singapore, one in six undergraduates living in a hostel was engaging in premarital sex. All these in conservative Singapore! In some surveys in the United States, 50% of teens have had sex before finishing secondary school! It is clear we are facing a crisis in this whole area of sex and sexuality. Yes, sex can be redemptive and healing, but only if it is within the marital relationship.

4. WORSHIP

Paul lifts the sexual relationship to the highest point possible. Before we look at his teaching, let us look at the evil Corinthian situation. To "Corinthianize" was an idiom that meant drunkenness and sexual immorality. There were 1,000 temple priestesses to the goddess, Aphrodite (goddess of love), who were sacred prostitutes plying their sex trade as part of their worship at night. Demonic bondage takes place when one gives his/her body over to fornication. These Corinthian priestesses were actually serving their gods through the use of sex!

I have counseled many men and women who have been involved in fornication or adultery. Fornication is the broader term for sexual immorality; while adultery focuses on unfaithfulness specifically to the marriage vows. Every time I find a demonic bondage which is more gripping than drug addiction. I have seen families devastated. Individuals struggle to break loose and cannot seem to find freedom. They need deliverance from this bondage. These individuals may find it hard to be faithful in marriage or to find true fulfillment sexually later on. They need healing in their spirit, forgiveness from

God, and finding their true identity in Christ. You need to see how terrible sexual immorality is. It brings demonic bondage. It breaks up marriages. It is hard to break free. Neil Anderson's book, *Bondage Breaker*, can be of real help in this area.

Let us see one more picture. A slave in ancient Greece belonged to a god of a temple. If he were going to become another man's slave, the prospective employer would take money to the temple the slave belonged to and redeem him from the god of that temple and pledged the slave to the god of the temple the employer worshipped in. So the slave either belonged to this god or that god.

Similarly, we either belong to the true and living God or Satan. We do not belong to the gods of this world. We are redeemed by God Himself. The word "bought" or "redeemed" literally means "bought out of the marketplace." We were bought up out of the marketplace of life where we were enslaved to the things of this world. We were freed to live for the true and living God.

Now let's take a look at what the apostle Paul teaches in 1 Corinthians 6:18-20. He teaches that our bodies are the temple of the Holy Spirit. We worship God in this temple. We glorify God with our body. All this is in the context of sexual faithfulness in marriage. Within marriage, the act of sex is an act of worship to God! Sex in marriage celebrates God's grace in bringing the husband and wife together. It is ministry to each other's needs, not because of earned favor, but because God has brought them together.

5. BUILT ON COVENANT AND COMMITMENT

Some think, "I do not need to meet my spouse's sexual needs if we have a disagreement or if I am angry with him (her)." But marriage is a sacred calling. According to 1 Corinthians 7:3-5, "The husband should fulfill his marital duty to his wife, and likewise the wife to her husband. The wife's body does not belong to her alone but also to her husband. In the same way, the husband's body does not belong to him alone but also to his wife." I am convinced that sex is a gift of grace—not only when all is well, or when you agree with each other on all matters. But no matter what, you seek to fulfill the spouse. In so doing the spouse will realize how valuable the marriage is to you, and will seek to fulfill you. Nothing should keep husband and wife from enjoying each other sexually well into old age.

Intimacy grows within the walls of protection. To believe that a marriage is a sacred relationship, based on a covenant with God and with one another, elevates marriage to its highest level: an expression of gratefulness to God for each other. It is a joy that God reserves for marriage—to seal the commitment that husband and wife have for each other. When a couple knows this, then sex is truly a fulfilling gift.

If, on the other hand, there are no sacred walls protecting the sexual pleasure a couple shares, then fulfillment through sex becomes a vain hope. Intimacy outside of marriage cannot be long lasting.

Realistically speaking, apart from the bonds of marriage, there is no guarantee for any married couple that their partner has reserved himself/herself strictly for the other. How does one know that the partner will not be unfaithful? Most who have more than one sexual partner will have several. This kind of relationship degenerates to animal passion. Animal passion by itself will die out.

Biblically sex is not a selfish getting, but an unselfish giving to fulfill the partner. Selfishness kills a relationship. Beyond that, if a married person pursues sexual fulfillment outside of marriage, he breaks the sacred covenant he made before God and man. Pray for all marriages to be powerful and successful. Married couples have their share of battles—and marriage is not easy.

6. EXPRESSES GRACE

Too often the marriage bed is used as a bargaining chip in a relationship."If you meet my expectations, I'll give you sex. But if you don't, too bad." Sex should be seen as a gift of grace that we minister to one another, whether deserved or not. There should be no conditions attached if a couple is committed to each other in marriage. It is a declaration of the gospel of grace, that God brings this marriage together, and that the couple is committed to God's grace in enriching the marriage. Grace simply means "undeserved favor." God loves us even when we do not deserve it. That is the exciting plus of marriage. Through our marriage, we declare God's grace and good news!

Better than any Christian or secular books on intimacy in marriage, Paul gives the wisest instructions for deepest fulfillment. First, in 1 Corinthians 7:3, he says it is a duty. We have a moral obligation before God to fulfill our spouse's needs in this area. Second, in 1 Corinthians 7:4-5, he states that the key is not to seek personal fulfillment but the fulfillment of the spouse.

The husband does not initiate sex primarily to meet his own needs but to help his wife find fulfillment, to know how important she is to him, and to free her potential. The wife does not enter the intimate times with the primary purpose of meeting her own needs but of helping her husband to become the leader in the home, to feel fulfilled as a man and to minister to his needs.

When my wife and I were students together in seminary, the prevailing wisdom of the time was, "men give love to get sex, women give sex to get love." While this may be true to a degree, Paul exhorts us to lift it to a higher level of unselfishness. We do not give to get anything; we give because it is God's nature to give. In return, we find deepest satisfaction and personal fulfillment! After all, it is in losing our life for Christ and the gospel, that we find it.

Grace is unselfish: Husband and wife are interdependent and belong to each other. They seek the best for each other, and in so doing find the highest level of fulfillment for themselves. Using another to meet our needs is selfish and builds on lustful desire. No one wants to be used as a tool for someone else's selfish pleasure.

7. ENJOYMENT GROWS

For couples who have resolved to walk together, work through their problems together, and serve God together, the joy of sexual intimacy grows through the years. Statistics gathered through survey after survey indicates that people with biblical views about marriage find the sexual relationship very fulfilling. Some may consider the biblical view "old fashioned", but it is God's design! On the other hand, those who seek after free sex and "liberated" lifestyles get tired of seeking joys in sex. It becomes mechanical and less satisfactory as the years go by. Those who think they are actually having more fun end up more frustrated and having less fun! Bible-believing Christians actually have more fun because they understand that God created the sexual relationship and we find the greatest fulfillment by following God's guidelines!

8. GUARDS AGAINST TEMPTATIONS

Satan would like to trap people in immorality (1 Corinthians 7:2). Fulfilling each other in the marriage bed is God's way for couples to guard against temptation. A single person may fight temptation differently and control his sexual drive in other ways. This is discussed in Chapter 5 *Singles: Focused and Fulfilled.*

Paul says that a couple should not deprive each other, except by mutual consent, and for a time, "so that you may devote yourselves to prayer. Then come together again so that Satan will not tempt you because of your lack of self control"(1 Corinthians 7:5). When a couple already find fulfillment in one another there is no need to pursue other means of fulfillment. That is why a woman should not deny her husband's needs but fulfill them. If she is not willing to meet his needs, it only causes the husband's eyes to wander and seek fulfillment in someone else. A wise wife knows the bedroom should never be a battleground.

A couple may fight over many things, but they should never fight over whether to meet each other's needs or not. Having such an attitude will help each one feel how important he/she is and how to meet the other's needs regardless. A husband who does not fulfill his wife may discover a wife who longs to be held, caressed, and cared for. He has a duty before God as the high priest over his family to offer a covering to protect his wife's emotions. We'll share more of this in the next two comparisons.

9. FREES COUPLE TO FOCUS ON SERVICE TO GOD

Paul teaches singles, "But if they cannot control themselves, they should marry, for it is better to marry than to burn with passion" (1 Corinthians 7:9). One of Paul's key teachings in 1 Corinthians 7 is the principle of least distraction.

Paul recommends that it is best to stay single, unless the sexual drives are so strong that they should get married. By meeting each other's sexual needs, it frees the couple to get past the passion issue and focus on service to God.

However, if those needs are not met, then one may be overly focused on the need for sexual fulfillment. This might overpower one's effective service for the Lord. Especially is this true for the married person who will feel deprived of his/her rightful due, and become frustrated in terms of sexual fulfillment as a married person. The cost to the kingdom of God is too great for us to be distracted from serving the Lord with our whole heart. We see major crises in marriage and morality today. Paul speaks clearly to married people: meet each other's needs!

10. Provides a Covering for the Family

"For the unbelieving husband has been sanctified through his wife, and the unbelieving wife has been sanctified through her believing husband. Otherwise your children would be unclean, but as it is, they are holy" (1 Cor. 7:14).

In the early church, many became Christians when their spouses were not. Paul does not tell them to divorce. Rather, he urges them to stay married and provide a covering for the children. Then Satan cannot destroy their family. Parents serve as spiritual gatekeepers. A gatekeeper is someone who guards against any harm upon the family. In order to keep Satan from attacking the marriage, or bringing generational curses upon the children, a healthy couple will put God first. They do so by loving each other. In this way, they offer a safe environment for the children to grow up in.

If either spouse comes from an abusive home, or one in which immorality or unfaithfulness reigned, the couple can become gatekeepers to keep that sin from hurting the children. My wife's father had two wives. It caused untold pain to her mother and to the children. But by having a solid marriage, my wife and I have broken any generational curses that may have been inflicted upon our children. They had the privilege and joy of growing up in a happy, secure home environment. But if there is unfaithfulness on the part of husband or wife, it shoots holes into the covering. The children will fear long term commitment themselves because they saw how their own parents' marriage had failed. Some may even feel guilty, thinking that, for some reason, they are responsible for the parents' divorce. There is also a high possibility that they too will end up with broken relationships unless they are able to break the curse of their parents through the healing grace of God.

Joe X became unfaithful to his wife. Shortly after, his teenage daughter became pregnant with her boyfriend. Jim Y abused his wife. Their daughter also married an abusive man. Children of divorced families often end up divorced themselves. Jane Z was unfaithful to her husband. Her daughter grew up feeling she had to treat men the same way. We must understand that the actions of one generation influence the generations to come. We have a major responsibility to our children, and our children's children.

11. THE ONE FLESH RELATIONSHIP PICTURES CHRIST'S RELATIONSHIP WITH THE CHURCH

Paul does not have inhibitions talking about sex. In Ephesians 5:31-32, he talks about the one flesh relationship which is sealed in the sexual act of marriage. Then he compares it to the profound mystery of Christ's relationship to the church! Sex is sacred, a holy act of commitment to one's spouse, a celebration of how Christ loved the church unconditionally and how the church submits to Christ. He is the bridegroom and we, the church, are the bride.

Paul says, "For this reason a man will leave his father and mother and be united to his wife, and the two will become one flesh. This is a profound mystery–but I am talking about Christ and the church" (Ephesians 5:31-32).

What is the profound mystery? Paul is referring to "the two will become one flesh." He refers to the sexual act in marriage that seals the covenant relationship! This is a picture of Christ's love for the church and the church's submission to Christ! God desires intimacy to the highest degree with us! Clearly, God does not want this relationship cheapened and distorted outside of marriage.

Years ago a pastor queried as to why adultery seemed to be seen as a greater sin than murder or stealing. Of course all sin is wrong. Life is sacred, so murder is wrong. Stealing is taking what rightfully belongs to another person. But marriage pictures the most sacred event of all—Christ's love for the church! His unconditional love, His desire for intimate communion with His church is being revealed. And, since family is the basic unit of society, its breakdown brings devastating consequences to the society and future generations. No wonder God said, "You shall not commit adultery." No wonder much of the book of Proverbs is written to address the issue of immorality.

Satan was at one time the worship leader in heaven. Then he wanted to exalt himself above God. God had to punish him and cast him out of heaven. Satan does all he can to pollute the purity of sex within marriage. He debases sex to filthy, dirty, erotic meanings. He promotes unfaithfulness in marital relationships. He wants to destroy marriages, because true Christian marriage is a proclamation of the gospel of Jesus Christ!

Satan does not want us to glorify God with our bodies! He does not want us to picture the beautiful profound mystery of the relationship of Christ with the church. And he has succeeded to a great degree. Even Christians find it hard to talk about this area. And Christian couples often downplay the great value of sexual intimacy within marriage.

12. Eros Redeemed by Agape

There are several words for love in Greek. *Agape* is the word most understood by Christians. It is unconditional, sacrificial, unselfish, purposeful love. Jesus set the example of *Agape* by dying upon the cross. The Greeks rarely used this word. More common among the Greeks is the word *phileo*—family or brotherly love. *Philadelphia* means "brotherly love." It is a good, wholesome kind of love. A third word is *eros*. We get the word erotic from it and it refers to a sensual, physical kind of love. The question is: Is there a place for *eros* for Christians? Since Satan has distorted true love, all that the world knows about is erotic, emotional, sensual love that is selfish to the core.

I believe there are physical joys of marriage. Christians can enjoy the sexual act to a higher degree than even non-Christians. The scholars call this *Eros* redeemed by *Agape*. God's love makes room for the greatest enjoyment of sexual intimacies within marriage! It is the Father's delight for couples to enjoy sensual, physical love within marriage!

To put it simply, Jesus took back what Satan distorted. Jesus took away the shame, condemnation, and guilt. He placed the sexual relationship at the highest level possible and told Christian couples to enjoy this privilege to the fullest extent.

Some may ask: What about oral sex in the marital relationship? As long as both husband and wife are agreeable and enjoy that way of making love, the Bible speaks nothing against it. But they must both want and desire this method of fulfilling one another. That is where communication and communion come in. But outside of marriage, oral sex is wrong. It is sexual immorality. It is *eros*, an erotic form of sensuality the same as fornication, or sex outside of marriage. It can bring demonic, psychological, and emotional bondage as much as any sinful sexual act.

So many Christians have felt that sex was a dirty word. I remember as a teenager my youth pastor saying sex was not so important, and its primary use was for procreation. This was the view of Thomas Aquinas many centuries ago. As a result, many couples gave up making love altogether. This view actually denies the direct teaching of Scripture to fulfill one's marital duty to our spouse (1 Corinthians 7:3)! Then, people like Dr. Tim LaHaye (author of *The Act of Marriage*) and Dr. Ed Wheat (author of *Intended for Pleasure*) taught us that sex was meant for pleasure and enjoyment in marriage, not just for procreation.

Now I want to take sex to a higher level. Sex at its highest point is intended for worship–to celebrate the relationship God has given you and your spouse. It is an act of grace, of unselfish ministry, and of pleasure and enjoyment. Married couples should grow in this area of their marriage. Take time to communicate, to understand each other, and to minister deeply into each other's spirit. Let me summarize why I believe that sexual act in marriage is actually an act of worship to God!

1. Our bodies are the temple of the Holy Spirit. We must glorify God with this body (Corinthians 6:19-20).

2. Our bodies are to be a living worship to God (in all that we do) Romans 12:1.

3. Sex in marriage is redemptive, healing, protects from sin and Satan's temptation (Genesis 4:1).

4. Marriage is built on a covenant relationship with God and our partner (1 Corinthians 7:3-5).

5. The sexual relationship is an act of grace, to minister to the spouse's needs (1 Corinthians 7:3-5).

6. The one flesh relationship is a drama that pictures Christ's relationship with the church (Ephesians 5:31-32).

7. The sexual act is an act of celebration of God giving the spouse to you. Genesis 2:23 – Adam was so delighted when Eve was created. His expression "bone of my bone and flesh of my flesh" is a Hebrew equivalent of "Wow! That hits the spot!" Proverbs 5:18 tells you to "rejoice in the wife of your youth."

   Dr. Richard Dobbins, Assemblies of God psychologist and founder of *Emerge Counseling Ministries*, set me thinking about this whole topic, when he suggested in a seminar that spouses should worship God while they make love. This theme did not originate with me. I am only taking it a step further by showing how Scripture has been teaching this all along!

8. The same biophysical mechanisms used in worship are used in the sexual act in marriage. (Dr. Richard Dobbins' lecture at Western Pentecostal Bible College, 1981).

9. The devil counterfeits everything that is good.

   Sex becomes, as in the case of the Corinthian prostitutes, an act of worship to a false god. In fact, in the Bible idolatry and immorality are usually inter-related. False cults, such as the *Children of God* in the 1960's and the present day *Eastern Lightning* cult in China, have used sex to seduce people into their cults.

   Paul says, "Do you not know that your bodies are members of Christ himself? Shall I then take the members of Christ and unite them with a prostitute? Never! Do you not know that he who unites himself with a prostitute is one with her in body?" (1 Corinthians 6:15-16)

   According to Barrett, unite "is used in the Old Testament both for sexual union and in a religious sense. ...body is a neutral term in that it represents the human self at the point of decision. It may be the servant of sin, or the servant of righteousness. If one places his body at the disposal of a harlot...the body has taken the wrong turning, and becomes flesh...signifying human nature perverted...it has fallen away from God..." (C. K. Barrett, *The First Epistle to the Corinthians*. New York: Harper & Row, 1968, p. 149).

   Fisher comments further. According to Genesis 2:24, "the two shall become one flesh" is about the marital relationship.

"Cohabitation with a woman was held by Paul to be of such nature that it united the two so that they became one person. It was far from being a temporary physical union. … In Jewish practice, it was the act of sexual intercourse that consummated the marriage. If sexual intercourse is the true mark of marriage, then one who has sexual intercourse with a prostitute is in fact married to her." (Fred L. Fisher, *Commentary on 1 & 2 Corinthians*. Waco: Word Books, 1975, p. 94)

Whenever I counsel couples where a third party has entered the picture in a sexual way, I find a bondage that is worse than drug or alcohol addiction. Satan takes advantage of the unfaithful partner's gross disrespect of the sexual relationship to enslave him or her.

The same is true if one becomes addicted to internet pornography. Even though there is no actual interaction with the person in the photo on the computer screen, there is an addiction of the mind that puts one's thinking and emotions into bondage. The same would be true of young people playing around with oral sex. The book of Proverbs warns of the entrapment one gets into when playing loosely with sex. I recommend that you read the book of Proverbs through once a month, especially if you are tempted in these areas. God's Word is very direct in these matters!

10. Sex in marriage should crown the marriage relationship.
    It should glorify God.

I encourage couples to worship God during their lovemaking. Thank God for each other! Praise God for giving that person to you! It will enhance the couple's marriage and their lovemaking experience. Most Christian couples do not understand the profound place lovemaking has in their service for God. This is why I jokingly say, "If you must argue, argue about money, in-laws, "outlaws" and other misunderstandings, but whatever you do, don't argue about the sexual relationship in marriage! Sex is sacred. Most still operate only at the level of the physical joys of lovemaking. It is time to take this experience another level up to the great celebration God intended it to be!

I challenge singles to remain pure. There is a huge temptation, especially if marriage seems a long way away, to say, "I want to experience sex. I feel like I am missing something. Anyway, how can it hurt as long as I am sincere?" The Bible is not wrong when it speaks of a trap, or bondage, or defiling the temple of God.

Revelation 21:8 lumps sexual immorality with occultism, murder and all the worst sins that are punishable in the lake of fire. God takes this issue seriously! So should we. You may ask, "What if I have already been involved in premarital or extramarital sex?" It is not too late to repent; to turn in another direction. Ask God to forgive you and to bring healing and deliverance to your spirit and mind so that this bondage will not affect a future relationship. Commit your life to purity. God can bring wholeness and healing to you!

I call on all of us to rededicate our lives holy and pleasing unto God. We want God to use us to the fullest! God will not shortchange you! Keep looking to Him. He knows your needs. Put God first, and He can put you first! After preaching this series on sex as an act of worship, I met one of my church members. She bravely said to me, "this afternoon my husband and I are going to worship!" I said, "Right on!"

CHAPTER 4

Parents and Children Empower Each Other

Parents reflect the Heavenly Father and Children Minister to Their Parents!

Children, obey your parents in the Lord, for this is right.

"Honor your father and mother–which is the first commandment with a promise–"that it may go well with you and that you may enjoy long life on the earth."

Fathers, do not exasperate your children; instead, bring them up in the training and instruction of the Lord. *Ephesians 6:1-4*

Parents

Most who teach on the above passage focus only on the children's responsibility to obey their parents. But I must speak to parents first. The parent's role is all important. Parents provide a spiritual covering against spiritual attack. They provide guidance and nurture from the time a baby is born till their child reaches adulthood. They are the primary role models for their children. The role of Christian parents is not primarily to follow an Asian or a Western way of childrearing, though there are wonderful values in each. We are not just to follow a given expert's theory on childrearing.

On the drama of redemption we are here to represent Father God. By our actions we declare to the angels and principalities and all those watching our lives, "This is how Heavenly Father relates to His children." Paul says "For this reason I kneel before the Father, from whom his whole family in heaven and on earth derives its name" (Ephesians 3:14-15). Our whole understanding of fatherhood should come from our Heavenly Father.

Interestingly, scripture tells us more about the father's role than the mother's! Perhaps it is because most mothers naturally know how to spend time to understand their children and teach them. Perhaps it is because the father's influence in many homes is so lacking. Or perhaps the danger is, when the father tries to apply discipline, that he becomes angry and emotional. Delinquency and crime, behavioral disorders, emotional problems, and drug addiction are closely related to a poor relationship with father.

The father's impact on his children is of paramount importance. The male role model is crucial for sons to identify with and learn from, so they may know how to lead in the home. The male role model is crucial for daughters so they know how to relate to men in a healthy fashion and to see how a man thinks.

Both sons and daughters need the spiritual covering of the father. This does not mean the single parent mother is not able to provide this blessing for her children. There are many good male role models in the church. My father died when I was eight years of age. But I grew up in Sunday school and found many who could become my role models as fathers and big brothers. Ephesians 6:4 speaks expressly to fathers not to continuously provoke or make their children angry. In the Greek the verb "provoke" is a present imperative—*do not continuously provoke*... Anyone may at times have a brief moment of anger. But this should not be a habitual, ongoing thing. There should not be deep seated anger. Discipline mixed with anger sends the wrong message to our children.

Discipline should be combined with love, because that is how Heavenly Father disciplines us. Hebrews 12:6 says, "Because the Lord disciplines those he loves..."

On the other hand, the tools of childrearing involve "training and instruction of the Lord." The word for "training" means to educate and discipline. It helps the child set boundaries so he will not violate the laws of God and the guidelines for the Christian household.

Children need to learn boundaries. It makes them feel secure. It gives them a sense of identity. Even as a teenager goes through the identity crisis, he is kicking and sometimes appears rebellious. He wants to know where the boundaries are. When parents run from this rebelliousness the teen becomes more confused. If parents attack the teenager, provoking him to anger, the teenager fights back. What he really wants and needs is that his parents are there for him.

The word for "instruction" means training by word of encouragement, but may also include correction when necessary. This is just how Father God trains and disciplines us! He helps us know our boundaries, yet He loves us. He gave us the Bible to teach us and impart His nature to us. Sometimes He has to correct us and chastise us. But He does it all, not to get us provoked or angry, but so we may be teachable under His mighty hand. It is vital, then, that father and mother represent one voice when raising their children. They must be a team. If they do not speak with one voice, there is no covering for the children. Confusion arises. Satan can attack.

The father-mother relationship is a most important ingredient in childrearing. Do they model Christlikeness? Do they communicate well? Do they face their problems and resolve them in an effective manner? Do they build each other's esteem? Do they show unselfish love for each other? Whether they like it or not, their children will be a product of their example. They will likely even raise their children the same way they were raised. Parents need to understand Father God's love and then impart that to their children. So how does Father God relate to us?

He reveals His unconditional love and holiness

Many Asians grow up in a shame culture. I have heard my mother say to me, "You are not as smart as your brothers. If you are not a good boy, mommy will not love you!" When we visited neighbors, she would say, "My son is not as obedient as your son. And your son is more talented than my son." I did not have high self esteem.

Many children who grow up in a western culture also grow up with low self esteem. Parents do not always affirm their children and develop their self esteem. But God loves us unconditionally. Even when we fail He loves us. Even when we do not live up to His standard He extends His forgiveness towards us.

Through unconditional love our children will realize that they are approved by us. Every one seeks approval. All need to know that, even when they fail, they are loved. So parents must model unconditional love and forgiveness.

Father God is holy

He sets boundaries for our sake. That means He is not tolerant of sin. We must repent. He chastises those who are His sons, those whom He loves. As parents we must dare to discipline, but we must do it in a loving manner. We must not do it in anger or out of emotion. We discipline in order to develop the best in our children, to develop their fullest potential, and because we love them. If they know that, they will not be unduly angered.

He extends His covering and protection over us. We used to sing the song, "He brought me to his banqueting table, His banner over me is love." (from Song of Solomon 2:4 and Psalm 23:5). God is *Jehovah Nissi*–the Lord our Banner.

Parental covering is so important. Families are breaking down all over the world. When Christian parents work together, openly communicate, mutually submit, and pray over their children, they provide a covering against Satanic attack. If one parent is unfaithful, it leaves room for Satan to attack the whole family. If abuse takes place, a child may be scarred for a lifetime, missing the love that he/she so longed for.

If parents constantly fight each other, there is no unity to protect the children. If they do not agree on child rearing procedures the child does not experience the benefit of strong, united parental guidance.

But in a united, loving, caring family, the child grows up with high self esteem, good communication methodology, confidently faces the future, and makes friends readily. This covering recognizes the reality of spiritual warfare. This covering does not allow the devil to do harm to the family. We desperately need to renew the teaching of parental covering! I cover my wife and she covers me. This gives the angels cause to rejoice and inflicts pain on Satan's devious plans.

HE PLANS FOR OUR FUTURE

"God loves you and has a wonderful plan for your life." In Campus Crusade's *Four Spiritual Laws* booklet, this is law number one. This is the theme of Rick Warren's *Purpose Driven Life*, which has become a best seller worldwide. God does not just save us to leave us alone. He has a purpose for our lives and develops our potential to reach that purpose. Godly parents will think also for the future of their children. They will invest time in their lives now. They will model godly character and integrity. They will help their children to get the education they need. They will be there for counseling if their children need help.

He communicates to us. What an awesome God we serve! He sent His Son to earth to walk amongst us, talk with us, and then to die on the cross for us! He loved us even when we were yet sinners! He inspires people to write the Bible as God's revelation to us. He reveals Himself in the greatness of His creation! He takes time to listen to our prayers. He works miracles on our behalf. But what happens in many families? Fathers do not talk with their children.

When I was pastor of a Chinese church in San Francisco, California, I told our youth that the average father in America spends only about fifteen minutes per day talking to his children. I had several youth say to me, "that is more than my father talks to me. He only says hello in the morning, and good night when he goes to sleep." How sad! That challenged me to communicate with my children.

When our children were being born, I set a goal. I wanted to be the greatest influence on my children outside of Jesus Christ! I knew that this would not be the case. My wife is a very loving mother. She would spend more time and understand our children better than I ever would. She would be their greatest influence. Just the same, I set that goal so that I would take up my share of the parental responsibility.

Taking time to communicate gives children self esteem. It lets them know they are valuable. It helps them learn to think through their decisions. It gives them a sounding board. It lets them know also, that this is how God loves them. God cared enough to communicate in many ways with His family! When we spend time in good, healthy communication with our families we defeat the devil, and we build the family strongly for God. Begin when your children are very young. Keep at it when they reach their teens. They need you then, more than ever. If you have begun the communication early, the door will be open for you to communicate with them during their crucial adolescent and young adult years. If your children do not find godly affection in the home they will search for it through sex, gangs, or the wrong influences.

HE BUILDS OUR SELF ESTEEM

He tells us in His Word how much He loves us. He forgives our sins. He blesses us with every blessing in heavenly places by Christ Jesus. He sent His Son to die on the cross for us. He created us in His own image. He puts the past in the past. He gives us many promises in scripture.

Our children need affirmation. Blessings can overcome the curses of our lives. Those vitally involved in deliverance ministries will all say that, even after deliverance has taken place, inner healing needs to take place and self esteem needs to be built. This is one of the major points that Neil Anderson makes in his teachings on deliverance. When we find out who we are in Christ we can break bondages!

Two of my daughters both went through some tough experiences in secondary school. One of my daughters was told she would fail, would never make it to university, and should drop out of school. My wife and I rejected that. We blessed her. We spoke words of confidence in her. We loved her. She gained self esteem. She graduated from secondary school. When she graduated from university her professors thought she was one of the best students they ever had.

Another daughter was shamed openly in a class. The teacher wanted her to drop out, feeling she would fail that course and lower the overall grade average of the class. We blessed her. We tried to review her biology notes for her and explain the principles (even though we ourselves were not clear on the principles). We tried to make learning fun. She began to catch on. From a failure grade (F!), she passed that course with a distinction! (In the British system of schooling, that is one of the highest marks). She went on to university and finished it one year less time than the normal student. She now has a Master's degree!

HE UNDERSTANDS EACH OF US AS INDIVIDUALS

Proverbs 22:6 says, "Train a child in the way he should go, and when he is old he will not turn from it." The Hebrew idea of "in the way he should go" is "according to his individual gift or bent." In other words, each child is different. You cannot relate to all your children as if they were made from the same mold or cast in the same imprint.

You have to consider the value, worth, and personality of each child. Each of my three daughters is different. My wife and I were the youngest in our families, so we did not know much about raising children. We tried to raise our first child by a book the family doctor gave us. We threw out the book for our other two children! It just did not fit! We need to give our children enough time to know and respect their individuality.

HE EMPOWERS US

As many as received him, to those who believed in His name, He gave the right (authority) to become the sons of God (John 1:12). Jesus told His disciples to wait in Jerusalem and they would be clothed with power (*dunamis*: life changing power) from on high (Luke 24:49). Even so, earthly parents seek gradually to empower their children. We teach them how to think so they can make good decisions. We can help them with goal setting. We can train them according to their area of gifts and skills. Then we can give them room to make some mistakes so they may grow. We set them free for their future. Our greatest longing is that they can fulfill their potential for the glory of God.

Paul warns earthly parents not to exasperate their children. This is where love is combined with the discipline. We are sensitive to their feelings, we understand their perspectives. We talk to them. Why must Christian parents be so careful here? Because the devil seeks to destroy families by breaking down communication links between parents and children. So much is at stake in the children's upbringing.

Blessings can come upon many generations if we nurture our children carefully. If we disciple them and train them in the instruction of the Lord. The training and instruction are of the Lord, not of human preferences. We want to develop a Christlike character in our children. On the drama of redemption we represent Father God.

CHILDREN

Children have huge responsibilities in this great drama of redemption. They are considered full fledged actors and actresses. They can obey God and defeat the devil. They can see miracles happen. They are vital members of the body of Christ. How do they fulfill their role?

FIRST, Christian children are considered adult sons or daughters of God. The Greek word "huios" (sons) as Paul used it, applies not to children under tutelage, but adult children who have all the rights, privileges and responsibilities of being a full fledged son of God (Galatians 4:5-6). We call God "Abba, Father", the special term Jesus used to refer to His Father. Some have said that "Abba" can be translated "daddy."

We have an intimate relationship with our Father. He rejoices over us with singing (Zephaniah 3:17). Just as the father ran to meet his prodigal son (Luke 15:11-32), God the Father runs to meet us and welcome us back if we go astray. We are heirs of God and joint heirs with Jesus Christ. That means all the blessings of the Word of God are available to us!

Sometimes teenagers say, "my parents do not trust me." But your Heavenly Father does. And He dares to let you bear the family name! You are sons of God (John 1:12). You have authority and responsibility to glorify God on the stage of the drama of redemption. Your role is equally vital to any other person in the drama.

SECOND, children are to obey their parents in the Lord (Ephesians 6:1). This is a reference to the Ten Commandments. The first four commandments relate to God. This is the fifth commandment and heads the list of commandments related to man. It is at home that we first develop our character and personality. Obedience is not just a forced "yes, sir." It is not surrendering to physical abuse or irrational actions. It is a willing obedience, just as Jesus willingly submitted to the Father. It is "obey your parents in the Lord". We must do that which will glorify God.

Children must think through those things which are pleasing to the Lord. They must study God's Word. They are not to sin and disobey God's Word. They must seek to obey their parents in every area possible unless it conflicts with the teachings of God's Word. If God has a call upon their lives, they must obey God's calling.

At the same time, they must not manifest a rebellious spirit. They must listen to their parents' insights. They must give proper respect where it is due. Some children think that this command favors parents. But this obedience is for the good of the children as well as the family, and the kingdom of God. "Honor your father and mother ...that it may go well with you and that you may enjoy long life on the earth" (Ephesians 6:2-3 cf. Deuteronomy 5:16). In other words, honoring parents will lead to a full life of God's blessings!

Third, children are soldiers in spiritual warfare. They have a responsibility to declare to the principalities and powers that they are submitting to Christ when they willingly obey their parents. They trust God to watch over their lives. By obeying parents, children stay under their spiritual covering so Satan cannot attack the family. By obeying parents they learn God has an authority structure in the universe. He has an authority structure for families.

When children learn how that authority structure functions, they learn how to gain authority as well. If they have a rebellious spirit or bitterness toward parents, then they will not grow beyond that rebellion. They will be looking at life through their past hurts instead of moving on to face the present and the future. They will likely raise their children the same way they were raised. There is power and freedom in forgiveness.There is power in ministering love even when mistreated by parents. Great growth happens when children attempt to build communication links to their parents. Even if they are met with rebuff and disdain, at least they are learning to use the right tools for adulthood.

Fourth, children can help parents develop leadership gifts. By submitting willingly to parental leadership, children help parents perform the leadership function and learn how to become better leaders. Thus they have a responsibility to minister to their parents' needs as leaders. That empowers the parents, and, in turn, blesses the whole family. That angers Satan. When children understand the authority structure of leadership, they can become better leaders themselves as they mature. A good leader must first be a good follower. Leadership is a gift that followers give to their leaders. It is a gift that children give to their parents. When I have spoken at youth retreats I have often given a talk on *How to Raise Your Parents*. The essence of what I tell youth is that it is not simply the parents who have a responsibility in raising their children, but children have a responsibility to help their parents. They can help parents become leaders, help them understand a younger generation, and be able to communicate to that generation. They can make a very tough job of parenting easier on their parents. They can calmly show their parents how they have matured in their thinking processes and can make valid decisions. This will help the parents to set them free later on.

FIFTH, just as Jesus had intimate communion and communication with the Father, even so children need to learn communication at home. Many youth will say, "it is impossible to talk to my parents. They do not listen to me." That may well be the case. But that should not prevent them from trying to communicate. They can maintain a Christian perspective of love, understanding, communication and forgiveness. In learning to communicate to parents, children build tools of communication which they will use in their adult lives. They will not bear the curses that might befall them through inadequate parenting (bitterness, anger, frustration, unforgiveness). Rather, they can break those generational curses. They can move on to happy marriages and fulfilled futures. They can reach their potential in God!

SIXTH, children witness by their lives. Children have a responsibility to show God's unconditional love to their parents, to be Christian in all their actions. In so doing, they indicate their desire to fulfill the parents' directions (in the Lord) and to defeat the devil's purposes. Parents will then see that their children do care about them and their desires. This will become a witness to them if they are not yet believers. They thus witness to the fact that their ultimate trust is in God to watch over their lives. But in trusting God, they are not bypassing their responsibilities to their parents. In Singapore, we are seeing many parents come to know

Christ because of the respect and reverence their Christian children give to them. My mother became a Christian when she saw three of her sons come to Christ.

SEVENTH, by obeying parents in the Lord, children declare that their identity is in the Lord. Teenagers often face a major identity crisis as they grow up. They try to find who they are. They want to know if they have worth. They can find their identity in Christ. They are really trusting God, even when circumstances or decisions seem unfair. They will do what God wants them to do, in spite of how they might otherwise react. Then they will learn that sovereign God watches over their lives and cares about their future.

Honoring of parents is the first commandment with a promise (Ephesians 6:2). God desires that the family structure be strong. A united family is a powerful family. It begins with mutual submission. The parents' role in mutual submission is not to "exasperate their children, but to bring them up in the training and instruction of the Lord" (Ephesians 6:4). They are to pour their lives into their children. They represent Father God to them.

The children's role is to obey their parents in the Lord. I believe with all my heart that one of the greatest miracles in the last days is that of united families, of parents turning their hearts to their children, and children turning their hearts to their parents (Malachi 4:6). It will be a sign to angels and demons, pre-believers and believers: godly, loving, caring, empowering, and uplifting families are possible.

CHAPTER 5

SINGLES: FOCUSED AND FULFILLED

One is a Powerful Number

Paul's passion in life was to please the Lord. He was focused on establishing churches and the evangelization of the world. That is why he said to singles "I would like you to be free from concern. An unmarried man is concerned about the Lord's affairs–how he can please the Lord. But a married man is concerned about the affairs of this world–how he can please his wife–and his interests are divided" (1 Corinthians 7:32-34).

God calls us to complete commitment in fulfilling our roles in the drama of redemption. The stakes in this drama are high. It is the proclamation of the gospel to the ends of the earth. It involves defeating the devil. We must declare God's glory in our lives, in the church, in the world, and in the entire universe. That was why Paul was single. He had every right to be married. But he knew he could be more effective for God! Actually, not many women could handle Paul's emotional personality, his traveling, his facing constant problems, persecution and imprisonment, and his single minded vision. John Wesley was not married until he was 47. Later he separated but was not divorced. With his strong personality, relentless pace, and unstoppable vision of founding early Methodism and evangelizing America, it seems likely that John Wesley should have stayed single.

There are many advantages to staying single. However, Paul also faced the reality that many would struggle with their natural sexual drives (1 Corinthians 7:9). Many would be more distracted staying single. Marriage is the best choice for them. Paul teaches the principle of least distraction: Always put God first, whether single or married.

Five Challenges to Singles:

1. Be a Happy Single!

Being single can be a holy calling (1 Cor. 7:8, 17)! Indeed, singles do have the freedom, finances and energy to do much for the kingdom of God. Nowadays, up to one-third of young adults are not married. Some are single by choice and some by lack of choice. When you include divorcees or widows, nearly half of a country's population could be singles. This social phenomenon is worldwide, especially in the urban centers. Many singles are so involved in their careers they have little time to develop relationships with members of the opposite sex. Many in Singapore have indicated that they would readily cancel a date if their work calls for it. While most singles would like to get married, they don't feel pressurized to do so. Being single is more socially acceptable now. Most would rather stay single than be trapped in a bad relationship. Jesus and Paul were single. In fact, given the fact that many marry at a later age, most of our lives are lived as singles. This brings up new issues and breaks old presuppositions.

We used to teach that for every person, God has a special someone for them to marry. This was a wrong, unbiblical teaching in the first place! This comes right out of Hollywood! Even many pre-Christians presuppose that there is someone they are fated to marry! Thus, many look only for that special someone, or wait unduly, thinking they had not met the special person yet. If God has that "special someone", how do we know this is the one? Some who thought they had heard from God, ended up regretting their decision and later decided it was not God's will! I remember a fellow student at Bible college who met and married someone within six weeks! A few years later this couple divorced.

Remember: one is a whole number. You are complete as a child of God. We used to teach that you are not complete until you get married. "The Lord God said, it is not good for man to be alone. I will make a helper suitable for him" (Genesis 2:18). The passage does talk about the benefits of companionship but it does not say God created man incomplete! While the majority will eventually marry, one need not think he is second class if he is single. Yet, often relatives and friends pressure singles into finding a mate.

Being the right one is more important than finding the right one. You should strive to be a satisfied single before seeking fulfillment in marriage.

If you have self-confidence, feel good about yourself, and have a good sense of self-esteem, you will be able to contribute greatly to a marriage. From there one can make better choices about partners. But if you rely on a relationship to make you whole, you may be asking for problems.

When it comes to marriage, remember 1 + 1 = 1. One half plus one half equals big problems. Incompleteness plus incompleteness does not equal completeness!

2. Commit Friendships to Christ!

Dating is the first major step on the journey of marriage, so pray about your dating. Invite Christ to join you in your dating. Or, would you be ashamed to ask Him? Date in groups. Often couples find it easy to get physically intimate too soon when they are alone. You need non-pressured times to get to know each other.

Will your dating help you to serve God more effectively? Do both parties have serving Christ as the first aim of their lives? Dating can help one develop socially if both parties realize that getting serious, if at all, comes later. You cannot be serious about a person until you get to know him or her better. Pay attention to the discussion during dates. Does it involve the interests of both parties? Or is the use of "I" and the discussion of self pre-eminent? Can you really share Christian values and goals with your date?

Joe and Jane were young people who dated, fell in love, and married. Yet, their existence together has been just that: mere existence. Constantly bickering, they felt an increasing hopelessness. Their marriage was in trouble. Why? Each married out of personal pain. She hated her parents and wanted to get away from her parents at any cost. He suffered from deep feelings of unworthiness and insecurity. Both thought that marriage would solve their needs. They felt that it was real love. It was–love of self! Many marry today because of personal need: insecurity, loneliness, escape from problems, social pressure, or a warped interpretation of real love. But the Bible tells us about godly love that is giving, unselfish, and precious. Sadly, real love seems so scarce today!

Dating in the East and West

Dating is so different from a Western and an Eastern perspective. The philosophy behind dating in the West is far more casual. It is getting to know many people, but not making a total commitment until a later point. Common among Western young people is,

"How many people have you dated?" It is built on having strong "feelings" for the other person. It is built on "there is only one truly destined for you." Sadly, that approach has also included many experimenting with premarital sex. Cohabitation has increased 1150% from 1960-2000 (Dennis Franck, *A Single Perspective* in Enrichment, Winter 2004, p.11). This approach has rapidly increased in spite of the fact that couples cohabiting are likely to divorce. This approach obviously has not produced better choices and more stable marriages.

In the East, there are a variety of methodologies in dating. In India, many marriages are still arranged by parents, with or without consultation with the son or daughter. There are also "love marriages" where two people meet and make their own decision to get married. In many Asian countries, dating is the basic approach before marriage. But this dating approach is far more cautious and the relationship is treated seriously.

Common among Chinese is the approach of asking, "Is he sincere?" In certain Asian countries, it is common to ask for total commitment at the outset of a relationship, even when the man and woman don't know each other well. While the Western approach is too casual, the Eastern approach may seek to make serious decisions too soon, before one really knows the other person.

3. Keep Pure

People are marrying at a later age now. Key questions are: Am I missing something by not having sex? How am I to handle my own sexual drives? Do I give in to them? Do I feel guilty about them? In an age of sexual promiscuity—keep pure. God made sex. In its proper place, sex can be exciting and wonderful. Out of place, it is degraded to a manipulation of feelings, personalities and bodies. It is also selfish, unfulfilling, and always demanding. It leaves pain and mistrust in its tracks.

You are growing physically

Your sexual drives grow stronger. These emotions must not be confused with love. They need to be controlled now so that they can be creatively used for fulfillment in marriage. It is easy to let these emotions blind us to the faults of others and to fall "head over heels" for someone or anyone. Read 1 Corinthians 13. Read it again in another version of the Bible. Is there any indication that real love is merely blind passion or infatuation? Life lived to its fullest–abundant life–is impossible without God's love. The rush to physical intimacy is often an indication of an inability to communicate in other ways on real issues of life.

Remember your body is the temple of the Holy Spirit. You are not your own; you are bought with a price. You are not free to do simply what you want and follow your emotions. You are created to give glory to God (1 Corinthians 6:19-20). God created sex to be thoroughly enjoyed within the marriage bonds. Sex in marriage is a spiritual experience of worship and a celebration of God bringing two people together. It is meant to be a climactic experience after a process of "knowing" one another through communication and a communion between husband and wife. To seek sex outside of marriage is to debase sex from a godly, spiritual experience to a fleshly, selfish, manipulative experience.

Sex and sexuality are not to be equated. Sex is physical. Sexuality reflects the whole of our personality as male or female. It is how we view life, how we think, how we face problems, how we feel about ourselves. Sexuality is who you are and all you do as a man or woman. At the same time, you also have a normal healthy desire for relationship with the opposite sex. Thank God that He created you as male or female. You are alive, vibrant, and can feel emotions. Thank God that you are able to enjoy the full range of emotions. This is how God created you! Sadly, in an age of broken families or poor parental role modeling, not everyone is able to enjoy that full range of emotions.

To deny sexual drives and to think that they are sinful only make them harder to handle. Then, sexual thoughts become obsessive. It is like trying not to think of the word "elephant" for the next 10 seconds. The only thing you can think about is "elephant"!

FACING THE "M" WORD

Masturbation is rarely talked about, especially in Christian circles. Doctors and psychologists know that most people have masturbated, some more frequently than others. Men tend to have more struggles in this area than women. We lived in an oversexed society. Flaunting sex is prevalent in advertising, in movies, in music, and in dress. So then, how does one control his/her strong sexual urges?

First of all, you need to know that masturbation is not mentioned in the Bible as a sin. However, it can become sinful and controlling if one continuously indulges in it, views lustful images or fills the mind with lustful thoughts. Remember that your eyes can become a spiritual gateway. They can allow good, wholesome thoughts to enter, or, they can allow pornography and lust to enter.

Second, guard your calling as a child of God. Guard your ministry, your future, your family and your church. Do not think you are above temptation. We are all vulnerable. If you have sinned, repent, and renounce every sexual misuse of your body and receive God's forgiveness.

Third, receive God's grace. I have seen many people live in condemnation. One young man did not know what to do with his normal sexual drive and felt he needed deliverance from demons! Condemnation only tightens the noose around us. We end up feeling more guilty. Then we will indulge in masturbation more.To break the vicious cycle of bondage where masturbation controls us, we must start with God's grace and unconditional love. He made us with our sexual drives. He knew that mankind needed these drives to marry and reproduce. So, God will not condemn us for having strong urges. It is how we balance our lives, fill our minds, and grow in Christ that will help us to channel our sexual nature to the glory of God.

Fourth, live a life of balance. It is important to know that sexual problems are not primarily sexual in nature but are personality problems. It could be a lack of balance in one's life, pain in the past, lack of fulfillment as a person, a stressed out lifestyle, or seeking to fulfill one's needs in a warped manner. When people have sexual problems they may be lacking in self esteem and self confidence.

A balanced lifestyle, a growing faith, and healthy relationships will help to keep our sexual drives in control. Exercise regularly and eat healthy foods. A consistent schedule that allows time to rest, recreate and develop wholesome friendships with both male and female helps. Learn to appreciate a variety of personalities, talents, and friendships.

Finally, adjust your expectation levels. The will of God supersedes attractiveness, talent, wealth, position, and achievements. Sometimes our expectation levels are overwhelming. In Singapore singles often look for a potential mate who has the five C's: Cash, Condominium, Credit Card, Car, and Country Club membership. Or, they expect Prince Charming to just walk up to them and propose! Rather than the five C's above, I have listed seven C's below which are far more important to evaluate.

i. Communication.

Does this person have a basic ability to communicate, to talk through problems, to share feelings, and to be unselfish? Can he/she speak the truth in love? Can he/she talk as a mature adult to other adults? Genuine communication transcends superficial charm.

ii. Character.
Is this a person of integrity and principle? Is he/she still fighting through unresolved conflicts and pains from a poor family background? Is there rebelliousness or unforgiveness? Or, through all the tough times, has this person grown in strength and character?

iii. Confidence.
Self esteem is very important. If you know who you are, you can be more unselfish in sharing with others and facing problems. You will be more flexible in adjusting to changing circumstances and personality differences. When a person has matured to a healthy self confidence, he/she has the potential to exercise the tools and talents to build a relationship.

iv. Consistency.
Emotional maturity is important. Someone who is unstable, constantly changing in his/her opinions, interests and occupations may need time to mature. The experts say "self management" must come before managing of others.

v. Caring.
Some only know how to take from a relationship. This will degenerate. Others are able to give to a relationship. This enriches the relationship.

vi. Commitment.
Can he/she make a commitment and follow that? Marriage is full of challenges. It demands a lot of hard work. It requires a commitment to work at a relationship even when feelings are not always there.

vii. Christ.
It is important for a potential spouse to sense the same vision and values, and to submit to the same authority (God). Proverbs 18:22 says, "He who, along the way of serving God, finds a wife, finds

what is good and receives favor from the Lord." 2 Corinthians 6:14 says "Do not be yoked together with unbelievers." When I shared this message in Singapore, one of our singles said, "Oh, I think that I must now look for 12 C's—Your seven C's and the five C's that Singaporeans are looking for!" I surrender! If your expectation levels keep getting higher and higher, then it will be impossible to find a suitable partner. We need to change our perspective and see what is really important.

Singles need to be free to meet people, to keep their eyes open to the possibilities. When my wife met me, I only had one of the 5 C's–a humble, small, used car. What if she could not see beyond that? We cannot let worldly expectations narrow our vision or blind us! As our expectation levels continue to rise, it becomes very difficult to find a suitable partner.

I am not saying singles should lower their expectations. I am saying they need to look more to inner strength and potential. There are no "ready made perfect packages" out there. Strategies can be developed to grow that potential partner to what he/she could be. Some of the greatest possibilities are being overlooked because of the silliest reasons: too short, too tall, not handsome enough, not smart enough, not rich enough!

Singles should not let fear drive them away from potential relationships, to reject persons before knowing them. They should do group dating, and attend concerts, socials, retreats. Win pre-Christians to the Lord! Look for potential, not perfection. All of us are simply works in progress. God is still working on us!

There is a fairy tale of a princess who kissed a frog. The frog became a prince. For many of you I wish God would open the blind eyes so you may see the possibilities! At the same time, singles should not rush into a commitment. Cupidity is stupidity! Some get awestruck with infatuation. One person told me she could know in less than 24 hours if a man were the right one for her. Some seek a soul mate. Out of loneliness and a strong sexual drive, some leap desperately and find themselves trapped in a bad relationship. The pains of loneliness are more bearable than the agony of a marriage in constant conflict, bitterness and hatred.

Singles must learn to trust in a caring God, even if there still are questions. Heavenly Father has a purpose for each life. Live life to the full and focus on the glory of God! You have an important role to play in the drama.

PART 2

The Church

"His intent was that now, **through the church**, the manifold wisdom of God should be made known to the rulers and authorities in the heavenly realms."
Ephesians 3:10

There is a story told that, before the creation of the world, God and His angels were discussing God's plans to send Jesus Christ to die for the sins of mankind, and to ordain the church to fulfill the Great Commission. The angels knew Jesus had to die on the cross to forgive the sins of mankind. What they could not understand was God's plan to use the church to fulfill His perfect will of proclaiming the gospel to the ends of the earth. They protested, "What if the church does not fulfill the Great Commission? What if they fail you? What if they turn inward and selfish and fight each other instead of glorifying God totally? God, is there any provision for that? Is there a plan B?" And God, with a tear coming down from his eye, looked at the angels and said, "There is no other plan. The church will succeed."

CHAPTER 6

THE CHURCH IS GOD'S IDEA!

Do Church God's Way, and Touch Your World!

The church is paramount in the drama of redemption. It is through the church that God's glory will be declared in the heavenly realms. Paul had an amazing understanding of the nature of the church, even from the point of his salvation. And because he saw the genius of the church as God created her, he was able to tap into and effectively develop the church for the glory of God. A most important "ology" for pastors to study is *ecclesiology*–the study of the church. Properly taught, this study of the church will transform our ministry!

If pastors only see the church as a building, an organization, a place where religious rituals are done, or where people come to hear sermons, then we see basically a "come" structure. The Jewish temple was a "come" structure. People came to Jerusalem to be blessed, to receive teaching, to worship. The Jewish synagogue, on the other hand, was a "go" structure. Synagogues adapted to each community and culture. Synagogues developed openness to new ideas. They became the community centers for Jewish people worldwide. They became a key tool for Paul to win the world. With their openness to discussion they were free to see how Jesus fulfilled the Jewish prophecies of the Messiah and became our redeemer.

The church is essentially a "go" structure. Come that you may learn and be blessed. Then go so that you may touch family and friends and the nations for the glory of God! In this chapter I share five key concepts of the church that made the early church so vibrant and powerful.

FIRST, THE CHURCH IS GOD'S IDEA!

Jesus said, "... on this rock I will build my church, and the gates of Hades will not overcome it" (Matthew 16:18).

If the church were an institution initiated by man, it would have been doomed long ago. Most earthly businesses and corporations have a life cycle of about 50 years, and, if they renew themselves, may have hope for a number of years more. But think of it: the church has faced adjustments to thousands of cultures and language groups, often poor leadership or poor transitions in leadership, erroneous doctrines, persecution, internal splits, poor governance, and many different structural changes. Yet the church moves on!

Growth is taking place faster than ever before. More people are coming to Christ than ever. Nepal, a country which had only 25 believers in 1960, now may have close to 1 million believers! China, which likely had about 1 million believers in 1950, may have close to 90 million today. South Korea is 39% Christian. In India the church is growing at twice the population growth rate. Nigeria presently has about 50 million believers. Experts predict by the year 2050 there will be 123 million believers there! (reported by

Justin Long, in *Charisma* Magazine internet edition, "The World's 10 Spiritual Hot Spots" January 2005, pp. 1-6). Christianity is growing at a most rapid pace, often outpacing the population explosion in Africa, Latin America, Central America, and Asia. In fact, counting people of all churches (Protestant, Catholic, Charismatic, Independent, etc.), over 2 billion people worldwide lift up the name of Christ!

Beginning with a small band of cowardly, inept, stumbling disciples two thousand years ago, Christianity has grown to be the predominant faith worldwide! More people are coming to Christ daily now than at any time in the history of the world! Truly, the wisdom of God's plan for the church to win the world is being revealed to all the principalities and powers! The devil is being defeated! God is victorious! That is why I say the church is God's idea enabled by God's power, redeemed by Jesus Christ.

In Greek, the word church is *ekklesia.* It means "called out for a purpose." In secular Greek it could mean something general, like a town meeting. But when Paul used this term to refer to the church, he was declaring the church has been set apart for a holy purpose. Just as, in the Old Testament, the Hebrew word *qahal* is used to refer to the congregation of Israel, *ekklesia* refers to a specially called out group of people with a holy calling on their lives—Christians.

In referring to the people of God, a key word used 2000 times in the Greek translation of the Old Testament (Septuagint) and 141 times in the New Testament is *laos*, or people. We are the people (*laos*) of God! This is the word we get for laity. In modern times we have read an entirely different meaning into the word "laity." We think laity is to be distinguished from clergy, or the full time ministers. Thus, the full time ministers do the work of the ministry while the laity sit and watch. This is unscriptural.

The "laity" are the people of God who need to be set free to fulfill their ministries! Together, on the drama of redemption, we will show the wisdom of God by obeying His principles: witnessing to the lost, submitting to one another in the body of Christ, loving our wives, submitting to our husbands in the Lord, not provoking our children to exasperation, and obeying our parents in the Lord. In so doing, we declare that the devil is powerless and that his rebellion against God was foolishness.

Jesus said, "The gates of Hades will not overcome it (the church)" Matthew 16:17-19. The church is born in the midst of warfare against all the plans of Hades! The church is given the keys of the kingdom of heaven. We are God's representatives on earth! The people of God, in these last days, will triumph over Satan.

SECOND, CONVERSION TRANSFORMED PAUL'S THINKING ABOUT MINISTRY FOUR WAYS.

First, Paul realized he was a sinner saved by the grace of God. Later, partly referring to the time he persecuted the Christians, he said I am the worst of sinners (1 Timothy 1:15).

For Paul, salvation had totally turned him around from night to day. His goals, values, vision, ambition, and character were totally transformed. God had done so much for him; Paul could do nothing but pour out his life for the gospel in thankfulness.

Second, Paul developed a very high view of the church. He understood that to persecute the church was to persecute Christ! (Acts 9:4-5). The church was the body of Christ, His representative on the earth! He would understand, that to equip the church for her ministries was his highest calling. Later, in writing to the divisive and problematic Corinthians, he said,"You are the church!" (1 Corinthians 12:27).

This church, which was so problem-filled, later rose up to her calling in Christ, became united, and great revival broke out. They touched their whole region for Christ. When I came to Grace Assembly, God dropped a word of wisdom in my heart—"Respect the church, love it and do not hurt it." That word was crucial in leading a four generation, multi-cultural church with her unique history! The church, as God created her, is mighty and powerful. We need to tap her strengths.

Christian Schwarz has done major studies in church growth. He discovered that healthy churches grow. There are eight key areas of development of a church to keep a church healthy: empowering leadership, gift-oriented ministry, passionate spirituality, functional structures, inspiring worship services, holistic small groups, need-oriented evangelism, and loving relationships. Schwarz documents from his research, that when a church is growing strongly in these eight areas, it will grow numerically as well! His book, *Natural Church Development* (Carol Stream, Illinois: Church Smart Resources, 1998) is a must-read for every church leader.

Third, salvation, for Paul, was a calling to missions and apostolic ministry! God said to Ananias, "Go! This man is my chosen instrument to carry my name before the Gentiles and their kings and before the people of Israel. I will show him how much he must suffer for my name" (Acts 9:15-16). Salvation for Paul was never simply assurance of heaven. At his salvation, he heard the call of God to reach Jews and Gentiles. He knew people are saved to serve. His converts would understand their responsibility to share the good news to others as well.

Fourth, signs and wonders followed Saul's conversion. He was healed of his blindness (Acts 9:17-19). Salvation was always related to a miracle-working God. He sought God to continue to work in signs and wonders throughout his ministry. Indeed, God opened up huge doors of opportunity for his preaching through the miraculous. That is the heart of evangelism today. I took an informal survey, asking my congregation how many of them, either personally or in their immediate family, had personally experienced a healing or a miracle from God. One third immediately raised their hands. Miracles did not cease in the first century! God works miracles today!

Fifth, he knew he would suffer many things for the name of Christ (Acts 9:15). It was no surprise. It was part of his calling. The church faces persecution in more areas of the world than ever. Yet, she grows faster than ever.

THIRD, THE CHURCH IS EMPOWERED BY THE HOLY SPIRIT.

On the Day of Pentecost the Holy Spirit came upon all flesh fulfilling the prophecy of Joel 2:28-29. John the Baptist further prophesied that Jesus would baptize us with the Holy Spirit and fire in Matthew 3:11. Jesus commanded His disciples in Luke 24:49 to "stay in the city until you have been clothed with power from on high."

Jesus promised them power in Acts 1:8–"But you will receive power when the Holy Spirit comes on you; and you will be my witnesses in Jerusalem, and in all Judea and Samaria, and to the ends of the earth."

The church could never win the world by human strength. Its leadership was too human. The disciples had deserted Jesus at the cross. In fact, on resurrection Sunday, the disciples locked the doors for fear of the Jews, when Jesus came into the room to appear to them. But on Pentecost Sunday, the disciples began to realize their mission. They chose a twelfth apostle, Matthias. All 120 disciples were filled with the Holy Spirit and began to speak in tongues. They were empowered for witness.

Years ago, I read Harry R. Boer's book, *Pentecost and Missions* (Grand Rapids: Eerdmans, 1964). Though not charismatic in his theology, he noticed that there is no repeat of the Great Commission in the book of Acts. Yet the disciples won their world for Christ. The Great Commission is assumed in Acts, so there is no need to repeat it. In fact, even in Matthew 28:19-20 "going" is assumed. It can be translated, "As you go, make disciples". The Great Commission is not so much going as "make disciples". And Jesus' disciples did just that in Acts, empowered by the Holy Spirit. They spread the gospel to the ends of the earth and planted churches to disciple followers for Christ.

The early church actually stayed in Jerusalem even after the day of Pentecost. It was still a come structure. It took persecution to thrust them forth to Judea, Samaria, and Antioch. It took a courageous, Spirit-filled Peter to preach salvation on the day of Pentecost (Acts 2: 14-40). He and John affirmed that indeed God was moving among the mixed race of Samaritans in the revival in Samaria (Acts 8:14-25). He submitted to God's vision and witnessed to Cornelius and his household, Gentiles who had not been circumcised, nor followed Jewish traditions (Acts 10:1-48).

The *come* structure had become a *go* structure. It conquered every hindrance. Paul could say "I was not disobedient to the heavenly vision" (Acts 26:19). He could say, "I will not venture to speak of anything except what Christ has accomplished through me in leading the Gentiles to obey God by what I have said and done, by the power of signs and miracles, through the power of the Spirit. So from Jerusalem all the way around to Illyricum, I have fully proclaimed the gospel of Christ." Illyricum is north of Greece. So Paul had preached the gospel beyond Jerusalem to five provinces, Galatia, Macedonia, Greece, Asia Minor, and Illyricum in less than 15 years! Today, we are seeing a great harvest of souls around the world. Possibly 80% of the people coming to Christ from the non-Christian world have been won to Christ by Pentecostal/Charismatic believers. Church historians are proclaiming the Pentecostal/Charismatic movement as the most influential force in Christianity today. Over 600 million believers are in this category!

FOURTH, POWER FLOWS THROUGH STRUCTURE

Paul understood the authority structure of the universe. In Ephesians 4:10-12 Paul says "He who descended is the very one who ascended higher than all the heavens, in order to fill the whole universe. It was he who gave some to be apostles, some to be prophets, some to be evangelists, and some to be pastors and teachers, to prepare God's people for works of service..."

Jesus, who was at the right hand of the Father, came all the way down to die on the cross for us and then ascended to be at the right hand of the Father. His purpose was to fill the universe with the glory of God. His method was to equip the church through apostles, prophets, evangelists, pastors and teachers.

Earlier, in Ephesians 1:20 the Father "... raised him from the dead and seated him at his right hand in the heavenly realms, far above all rule and authority, power and dominion, and every title that can be given, not only in the present age but also in the one to come. And God placed all things under his feet and appointed him to be head over everything **for the church**, which is his body, the fullness of him who fills everything in every way."

Jesus, in descending and ascending, conquered over every spiritual power that was against Him. He has all authority in the universe. He conquered every force in the heavenly realms. No authority can stand against Him. In His resurrection He has declared victory over demons, sin, and death! He did it all for the church. In His ascension He gives gifts to equip the church: apostles, prophets, evangelists, pastors and teachers, to defeat the devil, fulfill His will and fill the universe with His glory!

There is an interesting parallel of Paul's teaching to the Great Commission of Jesus.

	MATTHEW 28:18-20	EPHESIANS 1:21-23	EPHESIANS 4:8-13
Macro *Jesus' Great Victory*	Jesus has been given all authority (28:18).	Jesus ascended far above all powers (1:21).	Jesus descended & ascended to fill the universe (4:8).
Micro *Church Equipped and Empowered*	Jesus empowers his followers to disciple nations (28:19).	Jesus did it for the church (1:22).	Jesus gives gifts to equip the church (4:12).
Macro *Church fulfills God's Plan!*	... to the end of the age (28:20).	His body–the fullness of him who fills everything in every way (1:23).	Fill whole universe (4:10) with the fullness of Christ (4:13).

At the *macro* stage, we see the eternal reality. Jesus has won total victory. He has been given all authority. He descended to the lower, earthly regions and ascended to the right hand of God to fill the universe with the glory of God. Then, at the *micro* stage we see what is happening on earth. Jesus empowers His followers to disciple the nations. His descent and ascent and conquering every spiritual power was **for the church**.

When he ascended to the right hand of the Father, Jesus gave gifts to equip the church. Then we move to the *macro* stage again. In the eternal redemption plan of God, Jesus promises to be with His followers to the end of the age. He is going to use His body, the church to fill the whole universe with the fullness of Christ! God's plan shall be accomplished! Power flows from the eternal, victorious Christ into the church, in order to touch the world, and fill the universe with Christ's fullness.

When the church is structured effectively to allow God's power to flow through her, the church will become powerful! But most churches have become come structures. Part of the reason for this is a misunderstanding of Ephesians 4:11-12. Earlier versions of the King James Version included a comma that changes the whole meaning of the passage (the New King James Version does not, nor do most modern translations). It has been called the "heretical comma."

Punctuation was not included in the Greek of Paul's day. It was not added till about the ninth century A.D. into the Greek manuscripts. With the comma after the word "saints" in Ephesians 4:12, the King James Version seems to say that the apostles, prophets, evangelists, pastors and teachers are to do three things: perfect the saints, do the work of the ministry, and edify the body of Christ! All ministries revolved around the pastor! Instead of focusing on the Word of God, prayer, and vision, the leader's energies are scattered. No wonder pastors are prime candidates for heart attacks and ulcers! When I pastored in Northern California, three of the top level executives at our district office had experienced heart attacks!

Without the comma after the word "saints" it is clear that the equipping ministries of apostles, prophets, evangelists, pastors and teachers have a primary role to equip the saints. It is the saints who are to do the work of the ministry and to edify the body of Christ! Every member of the body of Christ must find his ministry gifts and exercise them! Equip in Greek is *Katartidzo*. It is a medical term. It means to set the bones of the body in the proper place. When all the bones of the body are in their proper place the person is healthy and able to do what he is created to do. When each member of the body of Christ fulfills his function in the body, the church grows and the world is reached with the gospel! Thus, the equipping ministries are in the church to give vision, leadership, direction, training, and set the example. The body of Christ is to do the work of ministry: to disciple, to evangelize, to care for other members.

The equipping ministries serve as a spiritual covering to protect the church from spiritual attack. No matter how much pain and misunderstanding I may go through, I must protect the church of Jesus Christ! I must not give place to the devil! I have always held that as a standard in my ministry. God has always honored that and lifted me to a higher level of ministry!

The power of God is then able to flow into the church and empower the saints for ministry! Then the saints will minister spiritual gifts to one another. Then the saints will touch the world with the power of God! They will fill the universe with God's glory! They will declare, "God has won, and Satan has lost!"

FIFTH, THE LOCAL CHURCH IS THE HEART OF GOD'S PLAN TO WIN THE WORLD!

This was the heart of Paul's mission strategy and methodology. He planted the church as a living organism in each geographical region. From there he trusted the Holy Spirit to help each church to evangelize the whole region for God. Thus, he could plant the church at Corinth and trust that this church would reach the whole of Greece. By reaching Ephesus, he could shake all of Asia Minor for God.

By planting a church in each culture and region, he knew that church could adapt to its own culture and develop local leadership. Then he taught each church about ministering the spiritual gifts. The great Catholic theologian, Hans Kung has said, "You cannot understand the church apart from the gifts (topic of whole book by Hans Kung, *The Church*, New York: Sheed and Ward, 1968)." Who taught the Romans, the Corinthians, and the Ephesians about spiritual gifts? Obviously, it was Paul. Everywhere he went, he would teach the churches how to exercise the gifts of the Spirit.

Paul uses many analogies for the church. One of his favorites is that the church is a body. All the parts relate to the head and are to reflect the headship of Jesus Christ. Paul knew that each body is a living organism, capable of reproducing itself. If each member of the body understands his or her role, then the body will function in a healthy manner. And healthy churches grow.

Paul saw the church as a temple. Your physical body is a temple (1 Corinthians 6:19-20). The church of Jesus is a temple (1 Corinthians 3:16-17). Jesus Christ is the chief cornerstone in God's temple. The apostles and prophets are the foundation stones. Our bodies are to be presented before God as a living sacrifice (Romans 12:1). Paul wants to be poured out (picture of a drink offering being poured out—1 Timothy 4:6).

He is "confident of this, that he who began a good work in you will carry it on to completion until the day of Christ Jesus"(Philippians 1:6). In this verse, "began" and "carry it on to completion" are two Greek words picturing the beginning and ending of a perfect sacrifice. Our whole life is a sacrifice or worship offered to God.

Paul also used other analogies, but these are key to his understanding of church strategy. The local church is at the heart of God's plan to win the world. Plant local churches everywhere. The church is a living organism with great capacity to multiply and reproduce itself if it remains healthy. The church is a temple and the church consists of people willing to be living sacrifices unto God. We worship God by our entire lives. All of life is sacred in the drama of redemption. There is no delineation between sacred and secular. Everything we do is holy. Every action can be a prophetic act declaring that God has won and Satan has lost.

Structure is so important. When a corporation is structured properly, it has great potential. When a family is structured properly, it is powerful. When a church is structured properly, each member knows his role and fulfills it. The synergy that develops lifts everyone to a higher level of effectiveness. Then the power flows through the pastors to the members to touch the world!

CHAPTER 7

The Script

Paul Uses Five Key Words for Ministry

There are five key words for ministry in the New Testament: worship, fellowship, teaching, proclamation, and service. It is important to understand how these words relate to each other. The first two words picture who we are. The last three words picture what we do.

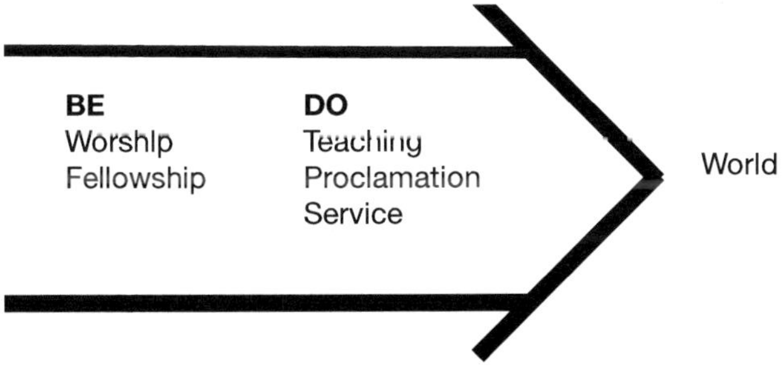

Worship

Worship and fellowship describe who we are. We are worshippers and we are a fellowship. Worship is not first of all what we do, but who we are. We are worshippers. That defines us.

1. Gives Him Glory

God created us to worship Him and give Him all the glory! My life is to be a spiritual act of worship (Romans 12:1, NIV). The King James Version translates "living sacrifice." But sacrifices are part of our worship. On the drama of human redemption we are worshippers. Our thoughts, our words, our actions are all on display for the angelic forces and demonic powers to witness. Our whole lives are played out on stage! I may do worship, but it is because I am a worshipper.

Pastor Jack Hayford said it well, "Worship is to God, but it is for you" (major emphasis of his book, *Worship His Majesty,* Glendale: Gospel Light, 2000). I would add, worship is to God but it is for you and for the church. God alone is worthy of our worship. It is an awesome thought. Holy God accepts you and invites you into His presence! He is our audience! We live out our lives on the drama for the audience of One, to glorify Him and hear Him say, "Well done, good and faithful servant (Matthew 25:21)."

2. Sees His Power

Worship is for you! We are privileged to come to the throne of God. There we see He is the Lord our Provider, the Lord our Healer, the Lord our Banner, the Lord of Hosts.We see He is God with Us, Wonderful Counselor, the Mighty God, the Everlasting Father.

All of these names of God are God's revelation to us of who He is, so that we may have confidence and faith in the all powerful, all wise, and ever present God.

He is the one who anoints us, heals our hurts, lifts us to higher motives, and prepares us to experience God and to receive His Word. He is the One who gives us energy and strength to face each new day. These are benefits for the worshipper! When we see God in this way, we are changed. We can never be the same again.

3. Reveals the Philosophy of the Church

Worship is for the church. The church is composed of worshippers. Our first desire and task is to worship God. The church is not a place for selfishness, divisiveness, pride, and greed. Even busyness on behalf of good works cannot take the place of worship. The worship service is the signature of each church. It is to tell the angels of heaven, the demonic forces and all pre-believers that this is what our church stands for. The worship service reveals our philosophy as a church, our direction, how we care for the flock. Others will see our love, our life together, and the God who is at work amongst us. Each worship service should incorporate the five key words of ministry. Note how we shape our worship services:

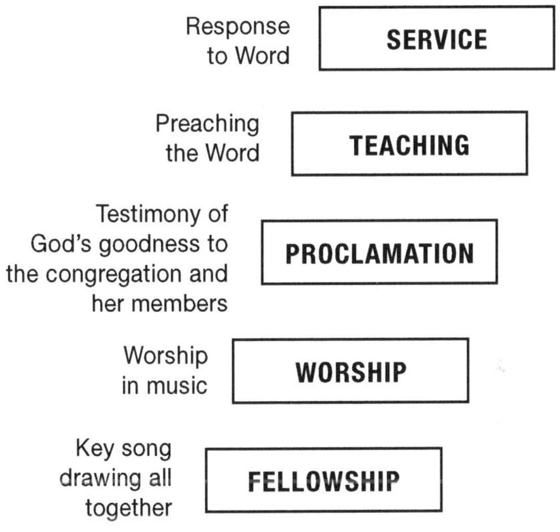

4. Releases Gifts

Powerful worship releases the gifts of the Spirit. God distributes many gifts to the congregation. Congregations that worship God freely usually have more of their people involved in ministries and in sharing of spiritual gifts. The reason for this is clear. Spiritual gifts flow out of relationship to God, praising God, and listening to God's voice.

Gifts are not merely human abilities and talents. When the Holy Spirit anoints our lives, the gifts flow incarnationally through us. When we realize the Spirit comes upon all flesh, then we affirm that every believer is valuable in the body of Christ. As self esteem grows, realizing who we are in Christ, we are more willing and courageous to minister spiritual gifts to others.

5. Empowers Evangelism

Powerful worship releases the church for worldwide evangelism. In fact, celebration may be one of the most important factors in evangelism for a local church. Eighty per cent of those coming to Christ from the non-Christian world are being won by the Pentecostal/ Charismatic churches. These churches are strong in worship. Why is this? Celebration renews our experience with the Lord. We freshly experience the reality of God in our lives. God who is above all (transcendent) is now right here with us (immanent)! We see God's greatness. Then we see His heart for the lost. Then we see the need to declare His glory to the nations! Worship energizes and empowers that vision.

When we speak in tongues (*glossalalia*), we are worshipping God. Everywhere in the New Testament, speaking in tongues is praising God. On the Day of Pentecost the crowd heard the 120 "declaring the wonders of God in our own tongues!" (Acts 2:11). At Cornelius' house "they heard them speaking in tongues and **praising God**" (Acts 10:46).

Paul writes to the Corinthians, "anyone who speaks in a tongue does not speak unto men, but **to God** (1 Corinthians 14:2); "if I pray in a tongue, **my spirit prays**...I will pray with my spirit, but I will also pray with my mind; I will **sing with my spirit**, but I will also sing with my mind... how can one who finds himself among those who do not understand say "Amen" to your **thanksgiving**.... You may be **giving thanks** well enough" (1 Corinthians 14:13-17).

6. Defeats Satan

Speaking in tongues edifies the person speaking. As we are built up in the inner man, we drive away demonic forces and claim God's victory! Sergio Scataglini is the pastor in charge of deliverance ministries for Carlos Annacondia, the famous Argentine evangelist. He believes those involved in deliverance should speak in tongues for at least an hour before attempting the deliverance. Since speaking in tongues is worship it builds the believer. He realizes his strength comes from the Lord. The devil was the former worship leader in heaven. He hates genuine worship. That brings in the presence of God. So worship is also key to our spiritual warfare as well as proclaiming the gospel to the ends of the earth.

Fellowship

Many years ago one of the biggest issues in church circles was, "on what basis can we have unity?" Church leaders recognized there were so many differences between churches, they were trying to find a common denominator that everyone could agree on.

Some thought unity could come around the communion table. But three views pervaded this discussion. Some felt the bread and cup actually turned into the body and blood of the Lord (Roman Catholic view), some felt the bread and cup were surrounded by the presence of the Lord when partaken (Lutheran view), and some felt the bread and cup were simply a remembrance of the work Christ did on the cross. Also, some felt only pastors or bishops should administer communion and others felt laymen could. That did not unite the body of Christ.

Some sought organizational unity. Protestants would not agree with the Catholics, so they formed a World Council of Churches and various National Councils of Churches. But the evangelicals felt they missed the whole point and formed the National Association of Evangelicals. The fundamentalists thought the evangelicals compromised on key issues and they formed their own council.

Some sought unity around the ordinance of water baptism. Again they found huge differences. Some sprinkled, some poured, some immersed. Some used the Trinity as the formula, others baptized in Jesus' name alone. Some did it once, some three times. Some churches made baptism in their local church a requirement for church membership, no matter if one had been baptized before.

Some tried to unite around a worship style. But then some liked high church Anglican music. Some liked Medieval Latin hymns. A few preferred the Puritan hymns. Yet others liked Hillsong or Integrity music. Some stayed with the hymns of the early twentieth century. Some preferred militant, prophetic songs. Others preferred soft, adoration type songs. Many articles have talked about the "worship wars" that various congregations go through, even splitting some congregations.

Obviously, these attempts at unity have failed. I believe that the bottom line is that Biblical fellowship and unity is based on one fundamental truth: we are sinners saved by the grace of God. All of us are sinners. We deserve nothing. Only God's grace can save us. The song goes "He paid a debt He did not owe, I owed a debt I could not pay."

The Apostle Paul saw everything as a result of the grace of God. His salvation, his spiritual gifts, his calling as an apostle, the church of Jesus Christ, the giving of an offering, even his sufferings were all because of the grace of God. Theologians have said rightly, "Paul's theology was grace and his ethic was gratitude."

What they meant was this. Everything in Paul's life was because of God's grace. Paul was so overwhelmed by God's grace. He knew he could never repay God. His only response would be a life filled with gratitude to God. He did not serve only because he had to, although he did say "For Christ's love compels us…" He did whatever he did as a thank offering to God. It kept him going in spite of the imprisonments, the beatings, the misunderstandings, and the persecutions. He said "give thanks in all circumstances, for this is God's will for you in Christ Jesus" (1 Thessalonians 5:18).

I myself marvel that God could use me. I was born in Bakersfield, California, in a non-Christian home. My brothers were smarter, more athletic, more talented musically than I would ever be. I was the youngest in the family. In secondary school I was always known as John's brother, or Steve's brother. In cross country races I would often be in the same race as Steve. The difference was, he was in the front group of runners, and I was always in the back! Humorously I would think "I'm behind you all the way, Steve!" What I meant was that I was way behind in the race.

After graduating from Bethany Bible College I joined Mr. and Mrs. Baird in a work among Chinese in San Francisco. I had to preach in English alone, because my Cantonese was so limited. More embarrassing was the fact that I had to be interpreted into Cantonese by the Caucasian missionary, Lula Baird! Her Cantonese was far superior to mine! The Assemblies of God, Northern California and Nevada District Council felt it necessary that I go to Hong Kong to learn Cantonese. I made many mistakes learning Cantonese!

Cantonese is such a language that, depending on the accent and tone you put on a word, it can mean nine different things. I remember once, instead of saying a woman's child was sweet and obedient, but because of the wrong tone, I called him strange. Then, we were called to pastor Grace Assembly. I would have to preach regularly in Cantonese, as well as English. I was following a senior pastor who was fluent in Mandarin, Hokkien, and Cantonese! I felt so inadequate.

Then, the church grew to beyond what I considered to be my organizational abilities. I had to restructure to bring in other gifts to the body of Christ. I cannot tell you every decision I made was good or even right. But God tells me, "I did not choose you for your abilities, nor did I choose you because you were the best person in the world for the job. I chose you because of my grace. This is the best place for you to grow. And you are my choice for this church." What awesome grace! How liberating! God, who knew all my inadequacies, choose me out of His unconditional love!

So we are a body of sinners saved by the grace of God. We have nothing to boast of in ourselves. We can dare face our sins and repent. We will not look down on others. But for the grace of God, there go I! We can step out by faith because we have nothing to lose and everything to gain. We are not here to build our own reputation or draw attention to ourselves. We can trust in God alone. We can reflect His love and grace to others because that is the solution for the world.

Somehow on the basis that we are a fellowship of redeemed sinners, the early church was able to overcome every obstacle and defeat every hindrance. What could have been utter defeat turned out to be great victory for the church! In the book of Acts we see that nearly every chapter contained some major obstacle that could have destroyed their unity, but rather led to the church growing more effectively. Let us take a look at Acts 6-15 and see how the church moved from a predominantly Jewish church to a church that became a Jewish-Gentile, multicultural church.

ACTS 6—FIRST CLASS MINISTRIES FOR ALL

Many overseas Jews (known by Hebrew Jews as Hellenistic Jews) became believers. They had stayed on in Jerusalem after Pentecost because it was the only church they had known and they did not want to leave. However, problems arose between the Hebrew Jewish widows and the Hellenistic Jewish widows. The Hellenistic Jewish widows felt discriminated against in the daily distribution of food.

The apostles did not feel they could bog down over such problems, nor did they feel they were the most capable ones to settle the problems. Yet, these were real, pressing needs. Peter spoke a word of wisdom. The Hellenistic Jews were to choose seven deacons from among them. They needed to be men full of the Spirit and wisdom, who had a good reputation among the Hellenistic Jews. What a wise move! These seven men understood the culture and language of their people. They were to administrate the daily distribution of food on a fair basis. If there were any complaints, this group of seven men would handle that.

They were given first class ministries. When we are **sinners saved by grace**, then it does not matter whether we are Jew or Gentile. Both are equally important in the body of Christ. The apostles could be free to minister in their calling and gifting. Great results came from this. First, "So the word of God spread. The number of disciples in Jerusalem increased rapidly, and a large number of priests became obedient to the faith" (Acts 6:7). Why was there such a harvest after such a decision? All the people saw how the early church loved each other, how they settled their problems, how there was no racial inequality, and how the spiritual gifts of wisdom and administration impacted them.

Why did a great company of priests become believers? If you study the history of the priesthood over the period of time from the interbiblical era to the book of Acts, you would find corruption, greed, and power politics in the priesthood. Some had even paid money to Caesar to be appointed high priest. It was a lucrative profession. And it was a shameful institution by Jesus' day. Jesus had even declared the temple a house of prayer, but they (the priests) had made it a den of thieves. A large number of priests saw how fairly the early church made their decisions. They knew it was both good and godly. They believed in Jesus! Beyond that, two of the deacons, Stephen and Philip became evangelists in their own right!

ACTS 7—STEPHEN'S BREAKTHROUGH SERMON TO THE SANHEDRIN

Stephen had been falsely accused by non-believing Hellenistic Jews of blasphemy. The high priest asked him about the charges. Most people do not realize the significance of Stephen's reply. They think he just recounted the long history from Abraham to Jesus just to prolong his life! But he addressed three key points in his sermon. The Jews had held three things most sacred: the Law of Moses, the Temple, and the Promised Land. Stephen attacked every one of those points. He said that God spoke to Abraham, Joseph and Moses *before* the giving of Moses' Law. *Before* there was a temple in Jerusalem, there was a tabernacle in the wilderness. God does not dwell in a house made with hands. Heaven is His throne and the earth is His footstool! And God spoke *outside* of the Promised Land! He spoke to Abraham in Haran, to Joseph in Egypt, to Moses in the wilderness. In other words, Stephen argued that the most sacred beliefs held by the priesthood of that day did not represent the essence of faith. God was bigger than their narrow thinking.

His sermon became the foundational sermon by which all Gentiles could come into the kingdom. They would come simply by faith in the resurrected Jesus who is the glory of God (Acts 7:55). Saul of Tarsus, who became the Apostle Paul, heard this sermon and saw the paradigm by which both Jews and Gentiles could be reached for God. The writer of the book of Hebrews forms his major arguments along similar lines. What an impact Stephen made with one sermon! I wish that even one of my sermons had an impact like that! While the Jewish thinking of that day leaned to exclusivism, pride, and narrowness, the early Church saw that God wanted sinners everywhere to repent and return to Him.

ACTS 8—PHILIP CROSSES OVER CULTURE TO THE SAMARITANS

Philip was a Hellenistic Jew. As a sinner saved by grace he knew he was most valuable to God. His calling was equally holy to that of Peter's. And he had no inhibitions of going to the "sinful

Samaritans" whom the Jews hated with a passion. God moved in signs and wonders among them and many believed. Philip then baptized many of them. But to maintain unity with the church in Jerusalem he called for Peter and John to come to Samaria and pray that they may receive the Holy Spirit, because the Holy Spirit had not yet come upon any of them (Acts 8:14-17). When we are sinners saved by grace, we value and protect the larger fellowship. We strive to be loyal and united in our efforts for God. In this chapter we also see Philip baptizing the Ethiopian eunuch without any Jewish preconditons.

Acts 9—Saul the Persecutor is saved!

Saul felt he did God a favor by persecuting Christians. This could have destroyed the early church. But God had other plans. Saul met God on the Damascus Road. Saul realized what a terrible thing he was doing. He was persecuting Jesus. Later, in 1 Timothy 1:15 he would say, "I am (present tense) the worst of sinners." He was partly reflecting back on this time of persecuting Christians. But he saw all of life as the grace of God.

The closer he came to God, the more he realized he was a sinful man. So, even after three missionary journeys, starting many churches and writing many epistles, he still said "I am the worst of sinners." The worst of sinners had met the grace of God! Paul could never repay God. Paul would preach the gospel in total simplicity and bring in thousands to the kingdom of God.

Acts 10-11—The Holy Spirit Intervenes at Cornelius' House

Peter was proud of his Jewish heritage. Certain animals were unclean to him. But through a vision God transformed Peter's views. God told him, "Do not call anything impure that God has made clean (Acts 10:15)." He was to preach the gospel to Cornelius. As a Gentile who feared God, he had interest in Jewish religion but would not engage in circumcision or any of the rituals of the Jews.

Peter realized from the vision that God was going to do a work among the Gentiles. Peter preached freely to Cornelius' household. Then, at a point that he might talk about becoming more Jewish, or following the Jewish rituals, the Holy Spirit interrupted his sermon. All of Cornelius' household were filled with the Holy Spirit and began to speak in tongues. Peter baptized them immediately.

When he was called back to Jerusalem (Acts 11) to account for his preaching directly to the Gentiles, he said two things. First, he recounted his vision and that God had said, "Do not call anything impure that God has made clean." Second, "the Holy Spirit came on them as he had come on us at the beginning… so if God gave them the same gift as he gave us, who believed in the Lord Jesus Christ, who was I to think that I could oppose God?" (Acts 11:15-17). The Jewish-Gentile barrier was breaking down.

Acts 13:1-3—The church at Antioch

The church at Antioch was a multi-cultural church. Five key leaders from five different countries are listed: Barnabas was from Cyprus; Simeon called Niger (presumably of dark complexion), Lucius was from Cyrene (possibly a Hellenistic Jew), Manaen was a Roman, and Saul was from Tarsus. No wonder it was such a missionary church. Here were people from different cultural backgrounds, working together and forming the platform for the strongest missionary church of that day!

Some church growth experts have argued for developing one culture churches (homogeneous), so that churches can grow faster. Granted, churches may grow faster when everyone is of the same culture and understand each other, but the early church saw great advantage in a multi-cultural church with multi-cultural leadership! When people see they are sinners saved by grace, racial color or background does not matter. Indeed they can learn from each other and expand their vision!

Acts 13–14—Paul's First Missionary Journey

The first missionary journey was a test journey. Paul wanted to see what God would do among the Jews and Gentiles in Galatia. It was a short trip, but a vital one. Signs and wonders took place and many believed in Christ, in spite of great persecution. But Paul wanted to test out his message and show that his ministry to the Gentiles was not in conflict with the Jerusalem church. Once the Jerusalem church would make her declaration, the door would be wide open to evangelize Gentiles everywhere.

Acts 15—The Jerusalem Council.

Peter spoke about God giving the Holy Spirit at Cornelius' house. They had the same experience as the 120 disciples on the day of Pentecost. Then Barnabas and Paul spoke of God working miraculous signs and wonders in the Galatian missionary journey. James laid down the scriptural basis in Amos 9 about God renewing David's fallen tent. Just as Jew and Gentile could freely worship God together in David's tent, so also, because of Jesus' death and resurrection, Jew and Gentile may freely come to God without discrimination. The result was the primarily Jewish Christian council in Jerusalem opened wide the doors of ministry to the Gentiles. What we see in many churches today is a modern tower of Babel. The original name Noah's descendants gave it was Tower of Balel (meaning Gate of God). They wanted to build a tower to reach heaven. Instead it became a Tower of Babel (confusion).

Faith leads to
Perpetuating culture to
Performance of Rituals to
Codes of Legalism to
Manipulation to make "nice churchmen"

Adapted from *A Theology of Church Leadership* by Lawrence Richards with Clyde Hoeltke, Grand Rapids, Michigan: Zondervan, 1980.

The above chart can be explained this way. The easiest and most dangerous thing for genuine faith is to degenerate to perpetuating a culture. Every church goes through about a fifty-year cycle, and either renews, or dies. From perpetuating a culture we move to performing a set of rituals that we consider sacred. Then we set up a code of legalism, a lot of do's and don'ts if people want to be accepted in that fellowship. Then we manipulate people to act like nice churchmen who know how to play the game well.

Actually, what should happen was modeled for us on the day of Pentecost.

Day of Pentecost
Faith leads to
Genuine experience that leads to
Allegiance. This leads to
Evangelism. As a result we have
Freedom to fulfill all that God wants for us

Adapted from *A Theology of Church Leadership* by Lawrence Richards with Clyde Hoeltke, Grand Rapids, Michigan: Zondervan, 1980.

On the day of Pentecost the Holy Spirit came upon the 120 disciples and all experienced speaking in tongues, an encounter with God that changed their lives. The early church was tightly knitted together in loyalty and allegiance to one another.

Acts 2:42-45 says, "They devoted themselves to the apostles' teaching and to the fellowship, to the breaking of bread and to prayer. Everyone was filled with awe, and many wonders and miraculous signs were done by the apostles. All the believers were together and had everything in common. Selling their possessions and goods, they gave to anyone as he had need."

This in turn strengthened their evangelism and "the Lord added to their number daily those who were being saved (Acts 2:47)."

The early church was free—free to worship, to evangelize, to minister gifts of the Spirit, to fulfill her potential in Christ! May it be so again today! This should be the picture of the church on the stage of the drama of redemption! Worship and Fellowship picture who we are. Teaching, evangelism, and service are what we do. Voluminous books have been written on each of these words. I shall briefly touch on them.

TEACHING

I summarize this role in five words: leading, feeding, discipling, equipping, and interpreting.

LEADING. Vision must be both taught and caught. If there is a great lack today in our churches, it is in the area of leading to the vision. Many pastors feel they do not have the gift of leadership.They spend more time managing. I have led pastor's seminars where the average size of the church was under fifty people. Yet those pastors said they did not have time to pray and to lead. They did not set their priorities correctly. One of the key functions of teaching is to lead God's people to God's vision for that congregation, to lift them to spiritual growth, until they also catch the vision for their own lives. The pulpit is the key place to cast the vision.

FEEDING. The whole teaching program of the church, from the pulpit to the classrooms to the cell groups, needs to nourish the people with relevant, life changing, biblical teaching. In a postmodern world where people question absolute values, the church needs to build a solid foundation so that the faith of believers will not be shaken.

DISCIPLING. All Christian teaching should have as its goal, to "make disciples of all nations … teaching them to obey everything I have commanded you" (Matthew 28:19-20). It is not enough to win people to Christ, our commission is to make disciples.

EQUIPPING. Take discipling one step further. Teaching is to equip people for their ministries. People grow when they find and exercise their ministries. The church grows when every believer is equipped. An equipped church will do her part in touching the world.

INTERPRETING. Just as Moses interpreted for Israel what God was doing at each event in her history, even so the pastor must interpret for the people what God is doing in the local church at that point of history. The pastor helps believers to understand what God is doing in their daily lives.

PROCLAMATION

The church is a "go structure." Her ultimate goal is evangelization of the lost. Jesus came first to reach the lost sheep of Israel. Paul was known as the Apostle to the Gentiles. The Holy Spirit broke down cultural barriers so that the gospel could be spread to the whole world.

The church was born in mission. The Bible is not the basis for missions. Missions is the basis of the Bible. "For God so loved the world, He gave his one and only Son…" (John 3:16).

The church can be structured to reach out. The church must be sensitive to the needs of people around her. A passion for the lost should be reflected in the overall strategy and planning of the church. Foreign missions must also be at the heart of any church. We need to develop Christians with a vision for the world.

Our church has partnered with Asian leadership to plant 505 churches in the past five years. We shape our cells to be community conscious, to build bridges to neighbors. We do many evangelistic outreaches each year. Our Chinese congregation use different strategies than our English congregation. We have a passion to reach the lost.

Soul winning must be in the DNA of each local church. The heart of God's plan to reach the world is the local church.

Service

The biblical word for service (*diakonia*) is the word for ministry. Ministry is the responsibility of every believer. Every believer should find and exercise his God-given ministries. In our church about 60% of those who attend have at least one ministry, whether to the church, or to the marketplace. We want every believer to be involved! Service also means we care about the total man. It is the arm of the church that cares for genuine needs and seeks to meet those needs practically, purely on the basis of Christ's love. It is the social consciousness of the congregation. Service is the Good Samaritan reaching out to the broken and bruised Jew. It is ministry to the hungry, the thirsty, the stranger, the poor, the imprisoned (Matthew 25:44, Luke 4:18-19). It is serving people in Christ's stead.

Service is an attitude of humility. We follow Christ's example as a servant. We are love slaves of Jesus Christ. We wait on tables. We esteem others better than ourselves. Husband-wife, parent-child, employer-employee and all relationships of the church are built on mutual submission and serving one another.

CHAPTER 8

SPIRIT BAPTISM: POWER THROUGH WORSHIP

Worship has been underrated in the Drama of Redemption

The cutting edge of growth in the Christian church is the outpouring of the Holy Spirit on all people. In the 1960's only twelve million had experienced a baptism of power that would change the face of the church worldwide. Now this number has grown to well over 600 million believers. What began as a trickle in the early part of the twentieth century has now become a mighty gushing river touching virtually every corner of the world. Speaking in other tongues accompanied this mighty baptism of power and it has changed individual lives, families, local churches and even whole denominations.

Most of the fastest growing churches in the world have experienced and are ministering in the gifts of the Spirit. The full orb of what God had intended for the church is now being revealed. The church is moving towards her potential and fulfilling God's plan to fill the universe with His glory!

Yet, most believers do not really understand the significance of speaking in tongues. Why did God give the gift of tongues? Some say tongues is the least of the gifts. Some say it is a gift that ceased after the first century. My wife's home church in Hong Kong taught that all you should do is to pray in tongues once in your life. Others put tongues down to emotionalism and ecstatic gibberish. They miss the significance of the gift of tongues. Another look at Acts 1:6-8 will reveal a unique empowering dimension to the baptism of the Holy Spirit. Notice three levels of faith in verses 6-8.

THE FIRST LEVEL IS FAITH BASED ON SIGHT. The disciples asked the risen Lord, "Lord, are you at this time going to restore the kingdom to Israel? (Acts 1:6)." The Jews expected that, when Messiah came, He would overthrow the Roman Empire's control over Israel, that He would establish Israel as a kingdom and that He would rule and reign on the throne of David from that day on. This was the most natural question. Now that Jesus had risen from the dead and proven to them beyond doubt that He was the Messiah, they expected to see the Davidic kingdom renewed.

Even so, many believers have a faith based on sight. As long as God meets their every need and agrees to their every desire they will serve Him. If everything goes well in their lives, they will gladly be His disciples. But if there is any tragedy, suffering, reversal in their situation or unanswered prayer, they will turn away from God. They are "fair weather Christians." They serve God when every prayer is answered immediately and clearly to their satisfaction.

THE SECOND LEVEL OF FAITH IS BASED ON TRUST. Jesus' replied to his disciples, "It is not for you to know the times or dates the Father has set by his authority" (Acts 1:7). Jesus clarified that there would be a delay before the kingdom of God is established upon the earth. Theologians call it living between the "now and the not yet." While the kingdom of God is now within us and we have power beyond our understanding, we do not yet have the fulfillment of all things.

That is why we still pray, "Your kingdom come, your will be done, on earth as it is in heaven" (Matthew 6:10). If God's kingdom had fully come already, we would not need to pray that prayer.

As Christians mature, they learn to put their trust in God, not in circumstances, nor in immediate answers to all their prayers. They learn to trust in an all wise God who is the same, yesterday, today and forever.

He is the sovereign God who holds the whole world in His hands. He watches over us. Not a hair of our head falls without His notice. He is our Heavenly Father. Delays are not denials from God but means to help us mature in Christ. In His time He makes all things beautiful. We know He is faithful. He is true to His Word.

THE THIRD LEVEL OF FAITH IS BASED ON UNCONDITIONAL WORSHIP. Jesus continues, "But you will receive power when the Holy Spirit comes on you; and you will be my witnesses in Jerusalem and in all Judea and Samaria and to the ends of the earth" (Acts 1:8).

Acts 1 and 2 are set in the context of the outpouring of the Holy Spirit on the Day of Pentecost. One hundred twenty disciples spoke in tongues. Three thousand people came to Christ. The church was born. A new people of God was formed that would declare His glory to the ends of the earth.

The Bible clearly declares the primary purpose of speaking in tongues is worship. In Acts 2:11 "we hear them declaring the wonders of God in our own tongues."

In Acts 10:45-46 Peter and his friends at Cornelius' house "were astonished that the gift of the Holy Spirit had been poured out even on the Gentiles, for they heard them speaking in tongues and praising God." Paul uses speaking in tongues as prayer and singing—worship (1 Corinthians 14:14-17)—"For if I pray in a tongue, my spirit prays, but my mind is unfruitful. So what shall I do? I will pray with my spirit, I will also pray with my mind; I will sing with my spirit, but I will also sing with my mind. If you are praising God with your spirit, how can one who finds himself among those who do not understand say "Amen" to your thanksgiving…?"

In 1 Corinthians 14:2 Paul says "For anyone who speaks in a tongue does not speak to men but to God. Indeed, no one understands him; he utters *mysteries* with his spirit." Do not confuse "mysteries" with "mysterious." Some teach that the devil does not understand the speaking in tongues and that it is our special secret code language to God. That is not true.

Paul says speaking in tongues are the tongues of men and of angels (1 Corinthians 13:1). Before the devil was the devil, he was an angel. So does the devil know angelic tongues? Of course. And does he know all earthly languages? Of course. Did he understand the tongues at Pentecost? Undoubtedly. Actually, the word "mysteries" in the New Testament means that which was hidden in the Old Testament is now revealed in Jesus Christ!

When we are speaking in tongues we are telling of Jesus' mighty attributes, of His greatness, and of His glory! I hope the devil understands everything I say when I speak in tongues because he will then cringe in fear when I declare God's greatness! The devil used to lead worship in heaven. The thing he fears the most is our worship!

Karl Barth said that when the humblest saint clasps his/her hands in prayer, the demons have to flee. When we worship God, we are declaring God has won and Satan has lost! So the primary purpose for speaking in tongues is worship. That is why Paul says "He who speaks in a tongue edifies himself…" (1 Corinthians 14:5).

As we worship God we see His greatness, His mighty nature working on our behalf. Thus, we are empowered. Tongues lifts us to the presence of a holy God. We begin to grasp the unconditional love relationship we have with the King of kings and the Lord of lords! In the presence of our awesome, holy God we see His magnificent provision for us. The gifts of the Spirit flow out of our relationship with God.

Learning to operate the gifts of the Spirit is not a matter of methodology but of relationship. It is in the presence of God that we find strength to fight the spiritual warfare and to declare God's victory and the devil's defeat. It is here we find hope for a new day in Christ!

When we understand the primary purpose of tongues as worship, then we shall see that the interpretation of tongues is either in the form of prayer and worship to God, or, an exhortation to people to see the greatness of God and a challenge to worship Him!

What passes for interpretation in most congregations is probably more a prophetic utterance. This is not to say there are no secondary purposes of tongues, such as intercession (Romans 8:27), and as a sign to unbelievers (1 Corinthians 14:22).

But we must understand the primary use of tongues and the essential nature of tongues. Tongues is far more than an outward sign. Intrinsically it is Spirit-empowered worship to God! The source of our empowering is Spirit-empowered worship!

God wants us to move into a lifestyle of worship. Focus on three concepts in Acts 1:8: power, to be, and witnesses. Look at the following diagram. Assuming that Spirit-empowered worship empowers us, you will see a cycle of power. Each ingredient enhances the other ingredients.

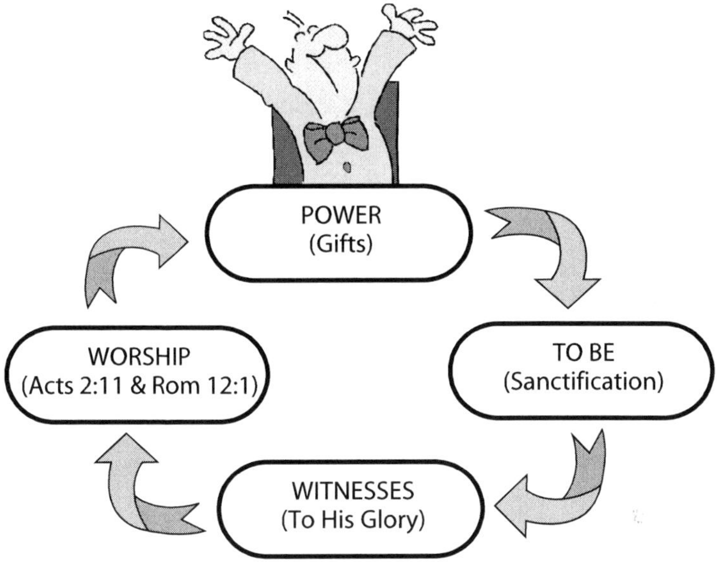

Worship Empowers
("But you will receive power")

The Greek word for power is *dunamis*. Some have referred to this as the dynamite power of God because the word dynamite comes from the Greek word *dunamis*. Because dynamite gives one big explosion of power and then is gone, I far prefer the concept of a dynamo. The power grows and grows. Why does worship empower us? Because it taps into the source of all power! God is beyond our sight, our intellect, our ability to understand.

The baptism of the Holy Spirit is not just an experience whereby someone says "I got it." It is the entry into a relationship. Clearly all believers have the Holy Spirit at the point of conversion. All the potential of the Holy Spirit is there. But Jesus prophesied that "Whoever believes in me, as the Scripture has said, streams of living water will flow from within him" (John 7:38). It is an actualizing of the potential. It changes the theoretical into the experiential. David DuPlessis, known as Mr. Pentecost across Christendom put it so well when he was asked at one university, "What is it that you have that we do not have?" He said, "We have the same. The only difference is that you have yours in the freezer and I have mine on the frying pan!" Speaking in tongues is Spirit-empowered worship to God! When we speak in tongues does this make us more spiritual? We need to demystify what speaking in tongues is. It is simply worship in a God-given language or dialect. Worship is plugging into the source. Our power is not a mystical power that makes us more spiritual than anyone else. It does not make us supermen and superwomen. It is like fuel for a car. It is God's empowerment of our lives.

To praise God fully is to know Him better. As you speak the wonderful works of God and declare His attributes, you are edified and empowered. When you praise God, you begin to transcend your circumstances. You become bold.

WORSHIP PRECEDES THE WARFARE

Then you find strength for the warfare. You see that when you fight God's battles, He does the fighting for you! Many people fight the spiritual warfare without first seeing the greatness of God through worship. They easily get discouraged and overwhelmed. The demons flee when we worship. Worship not only precedes warfare, it becomes a powerful weapon of our warfare. A worship lifestyle on the drama of redemption defeats Satan (the former worship leader of heaven) every time! In worship we declare prophetically the devil is defeated! One day every knee shall bow and every tongue confess that Jesus Christ is Lord!

WORSHIP SANCTIFIES
("POWER TO BE MY WITNESSES")

For many years the church has debated whether the baptism of the Holy Spirit is for sanctification or for power. Beginning in the

1800's a holiness movement arose that caused people to seek for a baptism of holiness. Men like D. L. Moody, A. J. Gordon, Charles Finney, and R. A. Torrey spoke of a baptism of the Spirit that was beyond the experience of salvation. The only problem was that it was not clear how to define the experience of holiness. How would one know he has been baptized by the Spirit? Then, around the turn of the twentieth century, God sovereignly poured out the Holy Spirit upon people of many nations. People were filled with the Holy Spirit and spoke in tongues. This was the beginnings of the modern day Pentecostal-Charismatic revival that has spread into the whole earth. Many in this movement took the Keswick Conference position on the baptism of the Spirit—that it was not for holiness but for power.

I believe the baptism of the Holy Spirit is both for holiness and power. We have seen the tragedies of great leaders who have failed morally and in other ways because their focus was on God's power instead of His holiness. The baptism of the Holy Spirit does not just give us a gift of talking to other people. It empowers us to become what God wants us to be. It is a lifestyle of worship to God.

The word "holy" reflects the nature of the Holy Spirit. God is holy. Beyond that, the biblical word "holy" means separated for a purpose. The purpose of the baptism of the Holy Spirit is to separate us and empower us for service to God.

One time several Pentecostal scholars and I were gathered together in a meeting. The discussion moved to whether the baptism of the Holy Spirit was for power or for holiness. Most of them took the standard position, that the baptism was for power, not holiness. Then I said, "What would you think of a position that the baptism of the Spirit is for vocational sanctification?" Vocational sanctification is an intellectual way of saying God sets us apart for our ministries! Suddenly several scholars eyes' began to get bigger.

It seemed to be a revelation to their souls! "Yes! That is correct! We have only seen holiness in the light of do not do this, do not do that. Do not get angry, do not lust." When we see holiness from the perspective that God sets us apart for our ministries, that is precisely what the baptism of the Holy Spirit is meant to do! We have the power *to be* His witnesses! We are talking about a lifestyle of witnessing.The following diagram best illustrates the biblical concept of holiness.

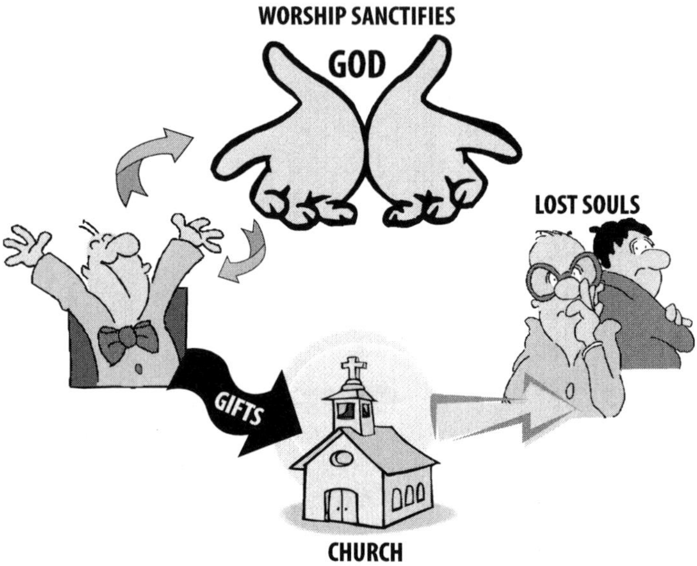

Holiness comes in intimate relationship with God. There we discover His awesomeness. We realize that we are sinners saved by the grace of God. We do nothing to deserve His grace. Yet He forgives us, cleanses us and sets us apart for service.

The closer we get to God, the more we realize our inadequacies in human strength. Yet He loves us. We want to be more like Him. We begin to take on His nature of holiness. From that intimacy with God, the spiritual gifts flow. Learning to minister the gifts is not a matter of methodology, but of intimacy with God. When we are in His presence, He drops words of wisdom and knowledge, faith, prophetic words and discerning of spirits. We begin to see His miracle working-hand in healing and in changing lives. Then we learn to minister those gifts to the body of Christ, the church. As the church is built up, she learns to minister in the power of the Spirit to the world. When we see how Holy God loves us in spite of our sins and shortcomings, we repent and receive His grace. We are overwhelmed by His grace and simply want to serve Him. We want to give our lives to God as a living worship (Romans 12:1-2).

Once that vertical dimension is established, we want to minister the gifts horizontally to others (Romans 12:3-8). When we pray in the Spirit, the Spirit dominates our thinking, our goals, and our lives. Then we are truly led by the Spirit. The more we worship God, the more we partake of His holy nature, the more our lives are changed into Christ's lifestyle. If we teach that the baptism of the Holy Spirit is only for power, then we will only tap into that power for certain areas of witness. But if we understand that God sets us apart for His purpose and thus makes us holy, we appropriate a lifestyle of holiness. Truly, we are empowered "to become" who God wants us to become.

Worship Witnesses to His Glory ("And you will be my *witnesses*")

We have all seen sad caricatures of witnessing: people with glum faces urge people to believe in Jesus or forcefully try to make people believe in Christ. During my early teen years I was privileged to go to the city jail and share my testimony with the prisoners. I jokingly say that through my high school years I was in and out of jail every week for three years!

The officer in charge of the jail went to my home church and graciously allowed me the privilege of going in to share the gospel every Sunday before church. I well remember one older preacher. Every Sunday he would say, "The world is getting worse and worse!"

and every week, he looked like he was getting worse and worse! Witnessing should not be negative or depressing. Witnessing is to tell others of the glory of God. When we share the gospel with a pre-believer, one on one, we should declare the goodness of God. We should not just speak the words, but we play the music of God's glory! Or, we may be visiting the sick in a hospital room. We are there to claim God's glory, wisdom and power on their behalf. Or, when we pray, we declare God's glory over families, situations, and nations!

Genuine worship may be the greatest impetus to evangelism. In worship we have a fresh touch from the Lord. We see God's mercies new everyday! In worship we see God's power and dominion. We begin to claim God's dominion in our own lives and in the lives of others. We dynamically claim "Your kingdom come, your will be done!" Then God begins to give us a vision to claim our workplace, our family, our neighborhood for God.

From strong worship we begin to flow into the supernatural. We begin to see God's healing power flow into people's lives. We have breakthroughs in our own lives. When we understand that worship is at the heart of the baptism of the Holy Spirit we no longer wonder, the baptism of the Holy Spirit is the key to breakthrough!

CHAPTER 9

Ministering Spiritual Gifts

Eight Principles of Prophetic Ministry

In this great drama of redemption, the church cannot be effective without God's power. The church around the world is growing effectively and rapidly. Signs and wonders are the cutting edge of the church as she reaches the lost.

I was preaching in Bangladesh not long ago. After making an altar call for salvation, I simply asked those who had just been healed by the Lord to come forward and testify. Dozens came forward! After a simple salvation message, God's hand was mighty to heal!

In countries like India and Bangladesh I have done informal surveys to find out how many had become Christians because they have personally experienced a miracle or have witnessed a miracle in a family member. Nearly 100% said they had!

In the area of spiritual gifts, excesses have always been a problem. Fear of misuse of gifts cause many to shy away from moving in this whole realm of spiritual gifts. We have all heard stories of people claiming that God told them to do something weird, or totally unbiblical. Perhaps they even bordered on fortune telling, or manipulation. The following principles are very important to ongoing ministry of spiritual gifts.

1. THE BIBLE TEACHES THE PROPHETHOOD OF ALL BELIEVERS

In the Old Testament the Holy Spirit only came upon specific individuals at specific times—prophets, priests, kings, judges. Joel prophesied that the Holy Spirit would come upon all people, male and female, young and old (Joel 2:27-28).That was fulfilled on the day of Pentecost (Acts 2:17-18). In fact, in the New Testament church both Jew and Gentile were anointed by the Holy Spirit. It was an anointing to see visions, dream dreams, and to prophesy. It was a prophetic anointing (Roger Stronstad, *The Prophethood of All Believers*, Sheffield: Sheffield Press, 1999). We have focused so much on the priesthood of the believer (a very necessary doctrine!), that we have overlooked the prophetic role of believers. This dimension is not taught in most sectors of the church.

The people of God should now be known as the prophetic people of God. Our lives should be prophetic. When people watch our lives they should know that we have encountered the living Christ, that we represent Him here on earth, and that we eagerly anticipate His second coming. The message of God's grace and unconditional love, of reconciliation and forgiveness, of God's holiness and glory, should be reflected in our actions towards our fellow man. When suffering saints in persecuted countries die willingly and joyfully for their Lord, they are declaring that the believer's victory is not in circumstances, but in Christ! When an employee is treated unfairly, but serves joyfully anyway, he declares that he is actually an employee of the King of kings and Lord of lords. When we proclaim Christ's dominion in our lives in spite of difficult outward circumstances, we declare we are citizens of a heavenly country.

2. Every Act in the Drama is a Prophetic Act

Since our whole lives are played out on the platform of the drama of redemption, and since good and bad angels are watching, the saints of years gone by are watching, and pre-believers are watching, every act we perform in the drama is a prophetic act. When we obey God's way and triumphantly claim His promises, we declare God's victory and Satan's defeat. Satan wants us to wilt under the pressure and heat of the trials. He wants us to surrender.

When the disciples cast out demons in Jesus' name, Jesus victoriously declared "I saw Satan fall like lightning from heaven (Luke 10:18)." Whenever we submit to God's way, we declare "Satan has been defeated (at the cross)! Satan is being defeated now (by my life)! Satan shall be defeated (when Jesus returns in kingdom power and glory)!"

No action, no word, or thought is insignificant in this cosmic battle. When we fight with God's weapons, there is power to "demolish strongholds. We demolish arguments and every pretension that sets itself up against the knowledge of God, and we take captive every thought to make it obedient to Christ. And we will be ready to punish every act of disobedience, once your obedience is complete (2 Corinthians 10:4-6)." Christ fills the cosmos with His glory—through the church! (Ephesians 1:23).

3. Prophecy is for Now—Live for God

Some say the gifts of the Spirit are not for today. They insist that 1 Corinthians 13:10 means that when the Bible was completed there is no more need for spiritual gifts. Nowhere in 1 Corinthians is there the remotest discussion of the completion of the Bible.

1 Corinthians 13:10 speaks of the day that perfection comes—that is clearly a reference to the coming of the Lord. But until the Lord returns, we need the spiritual gifts! Prophetic gifts tell us three things.

First, God is transcendent. He knows all and is above all. The future is in His hands, just as the past and present are! We need not fear the future!

Second, God is immanent. God speaks to us in the now. He can break into our lives at any point and speak life into us.

Third, we are the prophetic people of God. God speaks to and through all of us. Our life, values, actions, and words are to reflect His coming. We need to be sensitive to what God says to us through others. We need to be sensitive to speak into the lives of others so they will be built up and encouraged.

There are clear examples of people who have had prophetic ministries to this modern world. Mark Buntain was a great missionary to the poor of India. His life and ministry spoke prophetically of God's care and concern for the poorest of the poor. David Wilkerson went to the streets of New York City and proclaimed the good news to drug addicts and gang members. In addition, he often ministers prophetic words for the whole of the body of Christ.

I once was scheduled to preach at a church. But the program had been prolonged and I was allowed to preach with only about five minutes left in the service. But that was enough! Under the anointing of God, my message touched lives and people rushed to the altars. At another time, I had prayed long and hard for God's message for a church in Vancouver, Canada. I like to be well prepared. I received no impressions from the Lord. I wondered why. Then, as I was about to step into the pulpit, God gave me His message. For some strange reason, unknown to me at the time, the whole church responded to the message and came forward to the altar! Later I discovered that the senior pastor had just resigned that morning! The church was heartbroken and confused. My message ministered directly to their need! It showed them how much God cared for them.

Because God speaks to us in the here and now, our response must be to glorify God in all things. Prophecy can be for two purposes, to foretell and to forth tell. Whenever prophecy is used to foretell the future, it is to exhort us to a godly present. (The fancy way of saying this is that the apocalyptic indicative is followed by the prophetic imperative!).

In simple terms this means, when the Bible teaches us about the last days, it tells us how to live now. Most prophecy in the Bible is forth telling. It is speaking into our lives in the now. Indeed, most prophecies today are forth telling. These words help us confront what we need to do with our lives in the present.

4. THE GIFTS ARE INCARNATIONAL

Some teach that spiritual gifts are so supernatural that they have nothing at all to do with man. If the gifts are so supernatural they have nothing at all to do with man, why does God then use man? Why doesn't He use angels? And if gifts are 100% supernatural, then there is no way we can test them for error, or we will be guilty of doubting God.

On the other hand, some view spiritual gifts as little more than natural talents, dedicated to the service of God. But natural abilities alone cannot win the world for God! Both views miss the essence of Paul's teachings on spiritual gifts. A close look at scripture will reveal that God works incarnationally in our lives. There is God's part and man's part. Was Jesus Christ fully God or fully man?

Obviously, the answer is both. Jesus Christ was fully God and fully man. That is the meaning of incarnation. It is the false teachers who make Jesus either less than fully God or less than fully man. Is the Bible God's book or man's book?

The Bible is clearly God's Book, inspired by Him, and authoritative for our lives. But the Bible is also man's book. God used human instruments, their personality, vocabulary, purposes, and audiences to shape each book of the Bible. That is why we have four gospels, not one. Each gospel writer wrote with a different purpose and to a different audience. So, also, the spiritual gifts are incarnational. There is God's part and man's part. And because there is man's part the gifts need to be evaluated and tested.

Because the gifts are incarnational, we must realize that prophecy is not perfect. We must be understanding. We have all seen the excesses. A man prophesies to a woman that it is God's will for her to marry him. Someone prophesies that everyone should leave one church and form another.

I heard some "prophetic words" saying that famine was going to come to Canada so we should stock up on foods and prepare for tough times. That was over 25 years ago! Some prophesied that China would be open to traditional missionaries by August of 1994. Other prophets seem so accurate in one area and totally miss the point in other areas. One pastor prophesied that God's revival is coming under his anointing and all the other churches are to join him or miss out on the anointing. Other people who minister prophetically may succumb to moral failure. But we must not "throw out the baby with the bath water." The gift of prophecy, if tested properly, is a valid and valuable gift of the Spirit to be exercised until Jesus comes.

Firstly, the prophet is imperfect. No one is perfect. There may be hidden sin. There may be hidden agenda. Some may minister accurately at times and totally miss what the Spirit is saying at other times. Sometimes God gives me words for each person I pray for, sometimes it is the same word for all, and sometimes I get no words at all!

Secondly, communication is at best imperfect. We see but a poor reflection in a mirror. We may think we heard accurately, but what we heard may not have been what was said. I remember one time before I was married. I saw a beautiful bouquet of flowers in the youth hall of a church. I said, "How beautiful!" I did not know there was a young lady in the hall who overheard what I said. She thought I was referring to her! We need to give some allowance for imperfect communication.

Thirdly, we may have an imperfect understanding. Paul says, "We know in part and we prophesy in part (1 Corinthians 13:9)." Usually when I minister into people's lives, God does not give me the entire picture. He gives me a small part. We need to take time and not move hastily. We need to let others speak into our lives as well. We need to evaluate several prophecies together. Sometimes a message may build on, or confirm another. We must allow the Holy Spirit to either germinate the thought within us or we may confront a thought as not of God.

When I was but a child of nine years, I actually saw a vision which I thought meant that God wanted me to minister in China full time. I knew I had a clear call from God to be a pastor and to serve God full time. During all that time I looked directly to China as my ultimate goal.

Upon graduation from Bethany Bible College, I began to pastor a Chinese church in San Francisco. Then, strangely, my wife and I were called to Bible College ministry in Canada! I could not see how that had anything to do with going to China! After our ministry in Canada, the doors opened to become missionaries in a seminary in the Philippines which trained leaders from 15 Asian countries. Now, I pastor Grace Assembly in Singapore! I realize now, this is where God intended me to be. I have been to China, but China is still not open to traditional missions approaches. With our strong missions program here, I am able to touch all of Asia in ways I never thought possible before! My book on spiritual gifts has been translated into Chinese, Indonesian, Vietnamese and Tamil. We are broadcasting by radio into China regularly, and doing whatever we can to train leadership throughout Asia. Indeed, God put China in front of me, so that ultimately I would be in Singapore! If God had told me Singapore as a young child, I would not have understood what or why. I would not have traveled along God's pathway, learning His lessons, maturing in His way, and developing my gifts as broadly as I have. God is a wise God!

5. UNDERSTAND THE PRINCIPLE OF CONFIRMATION AND PREPARATION

The gift of prophecy is primarily for preparation and for confirmation, not for guidance. Prophecy may prepare you for the future and confirm what God has already been saying to us. If we need guidance, we need a word of wisdom.

The classic example is found in the ministry of the Apostle Paul. The church at Antioch was praying to send Barnabas and Saul for their ministry to the Gentiles. "While they were worshipping the Lord and fasting, the Holy Spirit said, "Set apart for me Barnabas and Saul for the work to which I have called them (Acts 13:2)."

God had already called Barnabas and Saul for a special mission to the Gentiles. But they needed the church to release them in God's timing. The prophetic word came forth and confirmed that now was the time for them to go forth. It is important, when doing the work of God, that we work under a spiritual covering. Barnabas and Saul knew that.That is why they submitted to the leadership at Antioch to release them to ministry. We see again the Apostle Paul waiting on God's guidance. In Acts 19:21 it says "Paul decided (Greek: in the spirit) to go to Jerusalem, passing through Macedonia and Achaia."

In other words, he knew by the Spirit of God that he needed to go to Jerusalem. We see that further confirmed in Acts 20:22-23 "And now, compelled **by the Spirit**, I am going to Jerusalem, not knowing what will happen to me there. I only know that in every city the Holy Spirit warns me that prisons and hardships are facing me." Paul knew two things. God wanted him to go to Jerusalem. He knew that he would face hardships there. But he wanted to follow God no matter what. The prophecies in every city were that he would face hardships and imprisonment.

Interestingly we see a new prophetic utterance in Acts 21:4. "Finding the disciples there, we stayed with them seven days. Through the Spirit they urged Paul not to go on to Jerusalem."

What was Paul to do now? In two previous verses we find that Paul knew in the Spirit he was to go to Jerusalem. But the disciples at Tyre prophesied that he should not go! This seems so contradictory! He would need a word of wisdom for guidance. Then, Agabus, a man with a validated prophetic ministry came from Judea and prophesied that Paul would be arrested in Jerusalem (Acts 21:10-11). He did not try to tell Paul what to do. In fact, they finally concluded that Paul would not be dissuaded, so they said, "The Lord's will be done (Acts 21:14).

You may ask, is this not a contradiction in Scripture? How can the Holy Spirit lead Paul to Jerusalem and, at the same time, tell him not to go to Jerusalem? The answer is simple. As mentioned in the fourth principle, the gifts are incarnational. It is God touching man. The Holy Spirit had warned Paul in many places that he faced hardships in Jerusalem. None of his disciples would have wanted to see Paul imprisoned or to suffer more than he had already suffered. Their preferences got mixed up in the message. That is why Paul did not scold them. He knew their hearts were with him. They just did not want him to suffer and be arrested in Jerusalem.

That is why prophetic words need to be tested and evaluated. They may prepare us for something in the future, or confirm what God has already spoken to us. John says, "Dear friends, do not believe every spirit, but test the spirits to see whether they are from God, because many false prophets have gone out into the world (1 John 4:1)."

6. FOCUS ON THE PROCESS

There are four elements to the exercise of gifts in the church. There is the sharer, the church, the utterance, and the results. We need to look at each in turn.

The sharer is part of his message. God speaks through a person. We need to evaluate. What is the messenger experiencing? What is happening in his life? What is he really saying? Is he speaking as a victorious Christian, or one struggling with major trials and hurts in his life? Is his spirit and attitude right?

The church is the context. What is God doing in the church at this point? Are the words that are being shared consistent with God's calling upon that church? For example, if the church is full of elderly people, it is not likely that God would be calling them to reach teenagers as a primary ministry. Every church is called by God to walk a certain pathway and each church is at a different level of maturity. We need to sense what God has been saying to that church and whether the utterances shared relate to what God is doing there.

The actual utterance is important. We need to evaluate what is really being said. Is it biblical? Is it clear, not just mystical? Do other people sense that God is saying the same things? If God is sharing with one person, He is also revealing His truths to others. I knew someone who, whenever she prophesied, spoke in mysterious ways and generally led everyone to a spirit of condemnation or guilt. I asked her, "Who and what are you referring to?" She said, "I do not know. I'm just speaking what God tells me to share." I instructed her not to share further because it sounded an unclear signal and only brought condemnation on others. We are responsible to take what God gives us and share it in such a way as to strengthen, encourage, and comfort others (1 Corinthians 14:3).

Look to the results. Does the sharing build up or tear down? Does it edify? (1 Corinthians 14:4). Are unbelievers saved (1 Corinthians 14:24)? Will we all worship God as a result? Are all edified? Are people instructed? (See 1 Corinthians 14:24-26). The spiritual gifts are practical tools to build the body of Christ.

7. Prophecy is for Learning and Growing

We are all the prophetic people of God. Actually prophecy is the easiest gift to begin to share. In 1 Corinthians 14 the word "prophecy" (the understood language) contrasts with "tongues" (the language not understood). So "prophecy" is used to represent every gift shared in the known language. Thus prophecy could refer to a word of encouragement and comfort, a word of knowledge, a word of wisdom, or a revelation. Paul says "you can all prophesy..." (1 Corinthians 14:26).

If you are a beginner in this area of sharing prophetic words, let me make a few suggestions. First, listen in your spirit to what the Spirit seems to be saying in the entire service. View the service as an entire whole, and each part as contributing to that whole. God may be speaking through a certain song, or scripture, or thought. Perhaps the sharing of others in a testimony or prophetic utterance may fall in line and confirm what the Holy Spirit has been saying to us.

Second, you may not know that what you have is of the Holy Spirit until after you have shared. In that case, you can even begin with "I feel impressed that... or, sense this..., or, a certain verse comes to mind at this point." We can offer humbly that which we have to share for the whole of the body of Christ to evaluate.

Third, you will learn from each experience. Paul says, "For you can all prophesy in turn so everyone may be instructed and encouraged." (1 Corinthians 14:31) The word "instructed" means discipled.

There is a discipling in the area of spiritual gifts. As we share, we learn. We observe those who are in leadership over us. We watch those who have more experience in this area than we have had. The more you move in the area of prophetic words, the easier it will be to share. You will grow in effectiveness.

8. Have an Eager and Teachable Spirit

Only the Bible is absolutely true. If we are teachable we can learn to make prophetic words a normal part of our lives. The great danger is that we think we have a hotline to heaven and no one else hears as clearly as we do. Some become proud. They are like the Corinthian church, thinking they were more spiritual than others and received more revelations. They look down on others. They try to manipulate others to their point of view. One man prophesied to me. I corrected him on three statements that were not true. He just shrugged his shoulders and said, "I must say what God tells me to say!" We must be teachable so that we can be more sensitive to what God is really saying.

Why must we be teachable? Firstly, we know in part and we prophesy in part. What we may share is not absolute and final.

Secondly, Paul says, if another person has something to share, you may keep quiet and allow the other person opportunity. It is not absolutely critical that you share a revelation every time you receive one (1 Corinthians 14:30-31).

Thirdly, knowledge does not begin and end with you. The source is God and the glory belongs to God. "Did the word of God originate with you? Or are you the only people it has reached? (1 Corinthians 14:36)"

Fourthly, in ministering gifts we must be willing to submit to one another. We are accountable to the body of Christ, and especially to the leadership. Paul says, "For God is not a God of disorder, but of peace (1 Corinthians 14:33, 40)." The picture in this verse is that of a disciplined army moving ahead under directions of the leadership. In this drama of redemption, we shall utterly defeat the enemy. We are a Christian army, and we must march on to victory together!

CHAPTER 10

Know your role and the Gifts will Flow

Fellow Members, Prophet, Priest, King

Ephesians 3:6-21

When we know our role in the church, spiritual gifts will flow. Many Christians do not realize who they really are, and thus do not recognize opportunities for spiritual gifts to manifest themselves. At least four roles are pictured in Ephesians 3. Knowing each of these roles will liberate us!

You Are the Body of Christ

Ephesians 3:6-7 says, "This mystery is that through the gospel the Gentiles are heirs together with Israel, members together of one body, and sharers together in the promise in Christ Jesus. I became a servant of this gospel by the gift of God's grace given me through the working of His power." Everyone is in the body of Christ! You are part of God's plan to change the world!

We may have anointing for different ministries, but it is the same Holy Spirit who anoints Sunday school teachers, church custodians, cell leaders, board members, and pastors! The usher in the church is equally important to the Sunday school teacher! This is revolutionary! Everyone is equally important in the body of Christ! When Christians realize how valuable they are, self esteem rises and they are more willing to minister to others.

While all are equally important, that does not mean our responsibilities are the same. Some of us bear larger responsibilities than others. Leaders have to have the authority to lead. "The elders who direct the affairs of the church well are worthy of double honor, especially those whose work is preaching and teaching" (1 Timothy 5:17).

During a New Year's Eve service I had an inspiration. I wanted to ordain everyone for their ministries! People are not only called into "full time ministry" or to be "ordained clergymen". God calls people to the marketplace, the business world, the education world, the sports world.

But the genius of the early church was that believers wanted to set others free for ministry. They considered others better than themselves (Philippians 2:3).

Stronger members valued weaker members. The parts of the body that had more honor knew to give greater honor to the parts that lacked it. Because of these reasons, Saul the persecutor could become Paul the Apostle. Onesimus the unprofitable servant could become a bishop of Ephesus (according to church tradition). Thomas the doubter could become a missionary to China and

India. Mark, the young man who failed early, could later write the Gospel of Mark that would influence the writing of Matthew and Luke. Tradition says he fled naked when Jesus was arrested in the Garden of Gethsemane. He dropped out of Paul's entourage on his first missionary journey. But he became one of the most powerful preachers of the New Testament era! Later, Paul, writing from a Roman prison, says, "Get Mark and bring him with you, because he is helpful to me in my ministry" (2 Timothy 4:11).

1 Corinthians 12:27 reveals Paul's amazing attitude about the church: "Now you are the body of Christ, and each one of you is a part of it."

The Corinthian church was one fraught with problems. Paul had to confront immorality, legal tussles, divisions, issues of meat offered to idols, abuse of the Lord's Supper, super spiritual Christians who looked down at others, and a belief that resurrection was not necessary.

If I were the Apostle Paul, my tendency would have been to say "God, erase this church completely! Let us start all over again! This church has too many problems! There is no hope!" But Paul does not say that. He speaks God's truth into their spirit. "You are the body of Christ." And Paul loved the body of Christ. It was the key to Paul's strategy to win the world!

He faced years of problems with the Corinthian church. He wrote 2 Corinthians in pain and anguish to try to resolve the issues. He sent colleagues to try to work things out and went himself a second time (2 Corinthians 13:1). Finally, he was free to come a third time to Corinth. He wanted to take up a special offering for the poor saints in Jerusalem. Then he had planned to confront their issues. But when he came, he discovered a church in unity and revival. They had lived up to Paul's faith in them—they were the body of Christ! Paul stayed for three months and wrote Romans, his great doctrinal masterpiece. Paul's key point in 1 Corinthians 12 is that, though we have different functions, we are all equal in the body of Christ, whether eye or ear, hand or foot. God has put the body together, so we should not boast about ourselves nor look down upon others. We are to work in unity! Thus, if we are all vital members of Christ's body, then we are to minister gifts to others. We need to impart to others and we need their impartation to us.

What makes us members together? How do we develop unity? Is it similar worship styles, agreement on all doctrines, reaching an arbitrary standard of holiness, or agreeing to certain policies or documents? No, we are one because we are sinners saved by God's grace! I have a core sermon entitled "I'm Glad I'm a Sinner". Please do not misunderstand me. I do not live in sin, nor do I seek to pursue worldly aims. But knowing I am a sinner saved by grace means five things.

First, I am free to face myself. Most of us dare not take a good look at ourselves. We are blinded to certain weaknesses in our lives. But I know that Christ loves me, just as I am, without one plea. I say, humorously, my wife loves me as I am, but she has hope for me, too! I can dare to face my flaws because of God's love. I do not have to hide my flaws. Then I can grow to full potential. Of course, He will not leave me as I am, but will effect change in me.

Second, I am free to serve others. If I know I am a sinner, I cannot look down upon another because of his appearance, personality, culture, lifestyle, or taste. Rather, I see others the same way I see myself. Apart from the grace of God, there go I!

I remember as a teenager going to the local rescue mission on a Saturday night. That is a Christian outreach to street people and alcoholics. They held gospel services each evening and then gave a free meal for all who attended. The church people sat on the left side of the auditorium and the "sinners" sat on the right side. One day I decided to sit with the "sinners" on the right side. I sat next to a young teenager who had a small brown bag. He looked at me and must have thought that I was hungrier than he! Actually, I had just had a good home cooked dinner! He reached into his bag, brought out a brown over ripened banana, and offered it to me. I felt humbled. Here was a needy boy reaching out to help someone he thought was needier! I realized then that the essence of missions is one beggar telling another beggar where to find bread. We need to be free to love others, regardless of their background!

Third, I am free to fail and to succeed. I know that I will make mistakes and yet God loves me. "Therefore, there is now no condemnation for those who are in Christ Jesus" (Romans 8:1).

When I was a younger pastor, some came to me for counseling who would talk down about themselves. "I am an awful person, I make many mistakes." I used to comfort the counselee by saying he is a fine person and not as bad as he suggests. Later I reversed my approach to counseling. I would tell the person who berates himself, "You know, you are right! In fact, you are worse than you think you are!" When they have recovered from their shock, wondering whether they should have come to me for counseling, I share with them the teaching of Ephesians 2.

Ephesians 2:1, 11-13 tells us "that we were dead in our sins, foreigners, aliens, without hope, and without God in this world!" But, praise God, Paul does not stop there! He says, "But now **in Christ**, we have become fellow citizens with God's people and members of God's household! Jesus makes all the difference!

I had a dream once that I went to heaven and met the great saints. I first met Peter. I said to him, "Peter, you great preacher of Pentecost, three thousands souls came to the Lord after one sermon! Peter, I have preached to thousands, but never have I won three thousand souls in one day!" Peter looked at me and said,

"David, do you remember how energetic you were in preaching, perspiring and changing your shirts between services?" "Yes, Peter, how did I do?" "Frankly, David, the preaching was boring!" Then I met Andrew. I said, ´Andrew, you great soul winner! You are a master of diplomacy! You won your brother Peter to the Lord and convinced a boy to part with his lunch so that Jesus could feed the 5000. Tell me about soul winning!"Andrew said to me, "David, do you remember trying to witness to that man on the airplane?" "Yes, Andrew. Was I effective?" "David, you blew it–you made many mistakes."

Then I met the Apostle Paul, my hero. "Paul, aside from Jesus and my mother, I wanted to meet you more than anyone else in heaven! I have taught your epistles in seminary, I even wrote a book on spiritual gifts based on your teaching! Expound to me the Word of God!" Paul said to me, "David, do you remember when you were teaching my epistles in seminary and you said, 'This is what the Apostle Paul really meant?' David, this is not what I meant!"

And then I met Jesus. With knees trembling, I did not know what to do. Jesus approached me with a book in His hand. It was the Lamb's Book of Life. Jesus read from the book, "David Lim, washed in the blood of Jesus. Enter into the joy of your Lord!" Praise God.

There is no such thing as failure for the blood bought one. And even when we fail, God can turn it around for success. We are not truly free to succeed unless we are free to fail.

Fifth, I am free to have faith in God. When I know I am a sinner I cannot cling to my ability or righteousness. I can only depend upon God. I need all of God's provision for me. What a source of supply! Our problem is we say that we depend on God, but we actually trust in our own solutions. We must learn to trust God totally.

I am free to love God and others. It is hard for human beings to understand unconditional love. God loves me simply because He loves me. It is not for anything I may do for Him. I think of the wedding vows: for better, for worse, for richer, for poorer, in sickness and in health—why, that is the way God loves me! Thus, I too can dare to love God and others in this same way. I have nothing to lose because He loves me with such an amazing love.

When I lead marriage seminars I often speak of three stages of a relationship. First, there is the "tiptoeing through the tulips" stage where one wants to impress the other. There is fear of hurting the other person's feelings. One does not know how the other will react or respond. Second, there is the negotiation stage where some issues are discussed and worked through. Third, there is the full confrontation stage where the couple is able to be open and honest and face each issue until satisfactory resolution takes place.

When we come to church, we do not come to impress one another; we just come to praise the Lord. We can be open with one another and truly minister into the lives of others. This is the basis of true fellowship.

So by the grace of God (*charis*) we are all members of the body of Christ. Then we begin to flow in the gifts (*charismata*). The gifts flow from His grace. I believe healing is in the body of Christ—spiritual, mental, emotional, and physical healing. We can bear one another's burdens. We can join our faith together and agree for the miraculous. We can speak into one another's life. We can claim all the blessings of being the body of Christ.

YOU ARE THE PROPHETIC PEOPLE OF GOD

Notice I did not say "pathetic" people of God! Many Christians, because of their murmuring and complaining, seem rather pathetic. But we are God's representative on earth. We must rise to defeat every enemy! Ephesians 3:8-10 gives us two purposes:"to preach to the Gentiles the unsearchable riches of Christ, and to make plain to everyone the administration of this mystery, which for ages past was kept hidden in God, who created all things. His intent was that now, through the church, the manifold wisdom of God should be made known to the rulers and authorities in the heavenly realms…" Our two purposes are to preach to the Gentiles and to make known God's wisdom to the rulers and authorities in the heavenly realms.

To put it another way, we are all actors and actresses on the stage of the drama of human redemption. (Please see chapter one on the *Drama of Redemption* for a more detailed presentation of this amazing paradigm). The title of this drama is "God has won and Satan has lost."

On the one hand, God and the angels of heaven are watching us to see if we shall obey God in this drama. On the other hand the devil and his demons are watching us (the rulers and authorities in the heavenly realms) to see if we will rebel against God just like they did sometime in eternity past. The pre-believers are watching us as well.

By our lives we declare, when we obey God's wisdom, that God has won and Satan has lost! By our lives we proclaim prophetically what Jesus accomplished for us at Calvary!

By loving my wife like Christ loved the church, I am proclaiming the gospel, that this is how Christ loves the church! Through her submission, she is showing how the church submits to Christ. She trusts God to do His part and to watch over her.

We, as parents, are God's representatives to show Heavenly Father's unconditional love and holiness to our children without exasperating them. We act on His behalf and for His purpose! When children obey their parents in the Lord, they are declaring their trust in God to take care of their lives. They are staying under the covering of their parents so that Satan cannot attack them. They are helping to develop their parents' leadership in the home. Each of these acts of obedience comes from a free will that is dedicated to serving God.

Of course, we do not submit when something ungodly is taking place or where God would not be honored. I am fully aware of cases where spouses or children are abused. Submission is not suffering abuse. And submission is not suppression. Abuse and suppression do not glorify God. But the husband loves the wife unconditionally for Christ's sake.

The wife seeks to submit strategically her gifts, her views, and her life so as to draw the best out of her husband and help him to be a leader and a man of God. The submission is purposeful and powerful. We are in mutual submission to each other to declare the greatest mystery in the universe: Christ's love for the church and the church's submission to Christ.

My former colleague, and good friend, Roger Stronstad is an outstanding scholar. He has written a book entitled, *The Prophethood of All Believers* (Sheffield: Sheffield Academic Press, 1999). He makes the case that, in the New Testament church, the Holy Spirit anoints all believers, young and old, and that all of us form the prophetic people of God.

Joel prophesied of a prophetic anointing that would come on all flesh. Pentecost is the fulfillment of that prophecy. The Apostle Paul states that "you can all prophesy in turn so that everyone may be instructed and encouraged." The gifts of the Spirit are given for the whole body of Christ. I believe the restoration of the prophetic ministry to the church has come first of all to the whole of the body of Christ. While there are some with special prophetic ministries validated by their accountability to the body of Christ and to local congregations, these are not many. All of us can minister into each other's lives through the Spirit of God.

One of the greatest theologians of the twentieth century was Dr. Karl Barth. He said, "When the humblest saint clasps his/her hands in prayer, the demons have to flee."

Why did he say that? Is it because we are mighty intercessors? Or that we are so spiritual? Or that we have many spiritual gifts? I'm sure none of the above is the reason. Rather, in the drama of human redemption, when we clasp our hands in prayer we acknowledge the Lordship of Jesus Christ, and we bow before Him as the great victor! We declare Satan has lost!

I believe this is true of singing, kneeling, dancing, raising our hands, and laying prostrate before the Lord. Satan, the former worship leader of heaven, does not want us to worship! When we worship God, the demons have to flee! Every act I do on the stage of the drama of human redemption declares God has won and Satan has lost.

As the prophetic people of God, we do not take revenge or fight our battles the human way. We minister in the opposite spirit to defeat Satan. This means, instead of hating my enemy, I love him. Instead of being frustrated, I show patience. When people injure me, I can forgive. I can bless those who persecute me (Matthew 5:38-48).

Paul says, "The weapons we fight with are not the weapons of the world. On the contrary, they have divine power to demolish strongholds. We demolish arguments and every pretension that sets itself up against the knowledge of God, and we take captive every thought to make it obedient to Christ" (2 Corinthians 10:4-5).

St. Francis of Assissi put it well in his prayer:

> Lord, make me an instrument of your peace,
> Where there is hatred, let me sow love,
> Where there is injury, pardon,
> Where there is doubt, faith
> Where there is despair, hope
> Where there is darkness, light
> Where there is sadness, joy!
> O Divine Master, Grant that I may not so much seek
> To be consoled as to console
> To be understood as to understand
> To be loved as to love
> For it is in giving, that we receive,
> It is in pardoning, that we are pardoned
> And it is in dying, that we are born to eternal life.

When we fulfill our role as the prophetic people of God, spiritual gifts begin to flow through us. We will speak in tongues. The gift of tongues has been called the eschatological gift because Joel promised that, in the last days, the Spirit will come upon all flesh. On the day of Pentecost all 120 spoke in tongues. At Cornelius' house, all spoke in tongues (Acts 10). At Ephesus, they all spoke in tongues (Acts 19). Paul's prayer is "I would like every one of you to speak in tongues…" (1 Corinthians 14:5).

Speaking in tongues is primarily praise and worship to God. It is declaring the great attributes of God. That is why tongues edifies the speaker. When we worship the Lord, we plug into the source of our strength!

When we become Christians, the Holy Spirit is within us. Jesus said, "Streams of living water will flow from within him. By this he meant the Spirit whom those who believed in him were later to receive" (John 7:38-39). The potential to speak in tongues is available to all. As we praise God in our known language, God gives us the other tongues. His Spirit touches our spirit, to worship Him. Carlos Annacondia is a man mightily used of God worldwide, and especially in the Argentine revival. He teaches that those involved in casting out demons should praise God in tongues for at least an hour before attempting deliverance (Carlos Annacondia, *Listen to Me, Satan!* Carol Stream, Illinois: Creation House, 1998). In the midst of spiritual warfare, praise breaks through the bondage! Those involved in intercessory ministries need to spend much time speaking in tongues. Intercession can be burdensome and overwhelming, but as we balance that with worship and praise, we see God's victory!

Discerning of spirits develops as we are sensitive to what God is telling us in the midst of spiritual warfare. It is important to know whether something is from God, from man, or from the demonic. If it is demonic, God can give us words of wisdom to know how best to cast out the evil spirits.

Sometimes a person needs inner healing and forgiveness to bring the deliverance, sometimes deliverance frees a person to receive inner healing. Sometimes we may need to fast and pray for a season first.

People can be set free from the bondages in their lives.We can impart Spirit-anointed words into people's lives at just the right time that may be life-changing! We may edify, exhort, and comfort others.

You Are High Priests!

Ephesians 3:14-19 is a prayer. Paul says he kneels before the Father for us. In Paul's priestly ministry he prays that we may grasp the love of God! We all have a priestly role to play. The priesthood of the believer is a liberating, empowering doctrine. Every believer is a priest, not just ordained clergy! In fact, the priesthood of the believer was the paradigm that allowed all of us to realize we have gifts and ministries to perform.

1. We are priests with a mission

Paul saw himself in priestly service. The Book of Romans is not only the gospel of hope but his defense of his priestly service in the gospel.

His goal is found in Romans 15:16, "To be a minister of Christ Jesus to the Gentiles with the priestly duty of proclaiming the gospel of God, so that the Gentiles might become an offering acceptable to God, sanctified by the Holy Spirit."

His mission in life was to present the Gentiles as an acceptable offering to God. Missions was his life mission. This involved ministering gifts of apostolic leadership, signs and wonders, teaching, equipping, pastoring, and, indeed, laying his whole life down for the Gentile cause.

In Romans 1:11, he longs to see them, "That I may impart to you some spiritual gift to make you strong…" He felt "obligated both to Greeks and non-Greeks, both to the wise and the foolish" (Romans 1:14).

His priesthood to God was his grateful response to the goodness of God in his life. In fact, he says, "But even if I am being poured out like a drink offering on the sacrifice and service coming from your faith, I am glad and rejoice with all of you" (Philippians 1:17). He visualizes his whole life as a priest, his ministry as an offering, and his body and the church as temples of the Holy Spirit.

2. We are a priestly nation

Peter talks about believers as priests offering spiritual sacrifices (1 Peter 2:5). He further declares that "we are a **royal priesthood, a holy nation**, a people belonging to God, that you may declare the praises of him who called you out of darkness into His wonderful light" (1 Peter 2:9). So in declaring His praises, we shall worship God and evangelize the lost.

We are a holy nation, set apart for God's purpose, a fulfillment of God's plan in Exodus 19:5-6 when He desired all Israel to be a holy nation. To develop a holy nation brings out gifts of leadership, administration, and service.

3. We are priests who worship God together

One of our purposes is to hear from God together, to discern what God is saying to the congregation. We are to minister words of grace and forgiveness to those hurting and straying. Priests bring people into the presence of God. They help people understand the ways of God (words of wisdom). They help people understand the insights of God in their lives (words of knowledge). They help people find their ministries (Ephesians 4:11-13).

4. We are priests in the home

As priests in the home, we are to offer a covering of spiritual protection for our families. We seek to cover one another with the armor of God that will defeat the attacks of the enemy. We seek to model a godly lifestyle and impart life into our family so they too will rejoice in the goodness of God.

We are to release captives from the bondage of sin through prayer, proclamation, and godly living. We have a ministry of reconciliation, to bring men to God and to be peacemakers among men. Fulfilling the priestly role sets free all the gifts!

You Are Conquering Kings!

Paul prays, "Now to him who is able to do immeasurably more than all we ask or imagine, according to his power that is at work within us, to him be glory in the church and in Christ Jesus throughout all generations, for ever and ever! Amen!" (Ephesians 3:20-21).

Paul is speaking of the King of kings and the Lord of lords! He is speaking of the all powerful God who is at work in the church both now and forever. Throughout Ephesians Paul talks about the greatness of God which is beyond human comprehension. And our victory is in Him! We shall reign with Him! That's why I see in this passage our victory as conquering kings. We are not paupers, barely getting a blessing or two from God. We are heirs of God, joint heirs with Jesus Christ, and we should live in the victory that we have in Him!

Jesus is our soon coming king. Everything the church does is in anticipation of His return. The church, by definition, is the church in light of the coming of the Lord. We worship, serve, teach, evangelize, because Jesus is coming again and His plan for the cosmos will be completed! We minister gifts in light of His coming. We stand against Satan. We live righteously.

We shape our values and goals in light of His coming. Now we know in part, we share in part, we prophesy in part but one day we shall see Him face to face! The gifts are to be ministered now! One day we shall no longer need the gifts. The gifts are a foretaste of the full manifestation of the glory of God.

As conquering kings, we need to claim back the territory that the devil stole from us. We need to submit to God's way of doing things. Many Christians seem to have lost their victory. They have given over areas of their lives to sin and unforgiveness. They have become passive rather than proactive.

Christians have often let degenerating values of culture affect us more than the Word of God. Even Christian families have been attacked and divided by the enemy. It is time to say that enough is enough! It is time to draw the line and tell Satan he has no right to our lives, our families, and our churches.

As conquering kings, we purpose to declare His glory over the earth through worship, missions, and living victorious Christian lives. We exercise gifts of faith to believe for the miraculous, for people to receive healing from God.We will move ahead proactively in our evangelism and missions. We shall prophetically declare God's victory and Satan's defeat. We shall develop godly families that are under spiritual cover.

Martin Luther said: "We all have two conversions. The first is to come out of the world. The second is to go back into the world with the gospel." It is through the empowerment of the gifts of the Spirit that we can go back into the world with confidence.

We will take advantage of every opportunity to exhort one another, speak blessings into each others lives, protect the church from Satan's attacks, and begin to march ahead as a united army empowered by the Spirit of God and claim God's promises and purposes in our lives!

PART 3

The World

Adam and Eve were created in the image of God. Part of the image of God is co-rulership with God over His creation. Man was created for dominion! But man lost dominion when he sinned. Jesus had to redeem mankind from sin's clutches. He taught His disciples to pray, "your kingdom come, your will be done, on earth as it is in heaven" (Matthew 6:10).

Paul taught us that we shall judge the world and angels (1 Corinthians 6:2-3)! Revelation 20:4 tells us we shall rule and reign with Christ for 1000 years. The kingdom of God is the key theme of Scripture.

Jesus said, "… the kingdom of God is within you" (Luke 17:21). We are to reveal Christ's kingdom to the world! His kingdom will bring down Satan's kingdom! We must begin claiming dominion at our place of work, in the marketplace.

CHAPTER 11

The Drama moves to the Marketplace

Ordain Every Believer for Ministry

Romans 12:6-8; Ephesians 6:5-8

The platform of the drama of redemption is not just in church. The church is a school where we learn to perform our roles. When we worship God in church we declare the glory of God. As Spirit-filled disciples, we learn to minister spiritual gifts to others. Every believer is an actor or actress in this great drama.

When we leave church the platform moves with us. When we go home, the drama of redemption takes place there. Empowered by the Spirit we reveal the glorious gospel of Christ by the way we treat one another at home. And when we go to the workplace the platform moves with us as well. We must do everything God's way, consider all of life as holy, and prepare to serve the Lord!

I. Do Everything God's Way!

The Apostle Paul even makes the master-slave relationship a part of the drama of redemption. In fact, when slaves in the Roman Empire became Christians, they affected the whole empire for Christ. They did this, not by rebelling against unfair masters, but by living out the Christian life before them! There are few master-slave relationships in the developed nations of the world today, but the analogy could be made to employers and employees.

You may protest that this is not a valid analogy, because the master in Paul's day had virtual authority over the slave's life, and that is not the case in most employer-employee relationships today. But look at the principles. They are the same for a God honoring master-slave relationship or a good employer-employee relationship. To slaves or employees, he says: "Slaves, obey earthly masters with respect and fear, and with sincerity of heart, just as you would obey Christ. Obey them not only to win their favor when their eye is on you, but like slaves of Christ, doing the will of God from your heart. Serve wholeheartedly, as if you were serving the Lord, not men, because you know that the Lord will reward everyone for whatever good he does, whether he is slave or free." (Ephesians 6:5-8).

Note the following truths:

1. *Every Act is a Prophetic Act*

By submitting to earthly authority we demonstrate to angels, demons, and pre-believers how we obey Christ, our heavenly authority. We declare that, by obeying Christ, God will win the victory in every situation of our lives!

2. *God's Authority Structures*

By respecting and fearing earthly authority we show that we understand the principles of the authority structure of the universe. This empowers and frees leaders to be leaders. This empowers employees to tap into God's power in their lives.

3. *Modeling the Servant Spirit*
By obeying out of sincerity of heart, we reveal our servant spirit. We show that we do not have a rebellious spirit, or a spirit that seeks to undermine leadership. Respect of our covering of authority allows God's blessings to flow into our lives.

4. *Touching Our World*
We obey, not in order to win favor from the employer, or with eye service, as men pleasers. We obey out of a liberated spirit and no hidden agenda. We may be ill treated, but people will see that we are not lesser men and women for it. We rise above unfairness to be a witness for Christ. This is walking the second mile. In Jesus' day, Roman soldiers could compel a Jew to carry their luggage for one mile. Jesus told his disciples to walk the second mile. During that second mile they are able to witness to the joy of the Lord. There we can genuinely serve others sacrificially and freely. We are different. We think differently. We will make a difference!

5. *Attitude*
We may not even be slaves, but because we are love slaves of Christ, we do the will of God from the heart, willingly, cheerfully, and triumphantly. This kind of attitude will change the world!

6. *Motivation-Life on a Higher Level*
We are actually serving the Lord. Men simply act as earthly authority over us. We live in a different realm and with a different vision. This motivates us like nothing else can!

7. *Reward*
Even when there may be unfairness our trust is in God. He will reward us abundantly for doing things God's way. Every good we do will be rewarded. God is the judge. He is just and fair.

Mutual submission prefaces this whole section on relationships. "Submit to one another" (Ephesians 5:21). Even so, God's rewards for following the seven principles above are for both slave and free. Masters and employers benefit from these principles as well. Onesimus, an unprofitable slave who ran away from Philemon, found Christ in Rome and then was reconciled to Philemon. Tradition tells us that he later became the bishop of the great church at Ephesus! God is able to open incredible doors beyond anything you can imagine, if you are faithful to Him!

What does Paul say to masters or employers?

"And masters, treat your slaves in the same way. Do not threaten them, since you know that he who is both their Master and yours is in heaven, and there is no favoritism with him" (Ephesians 6:9).

These truths are for masters or employers to note:

1. HOLY CALLING. How are masters to treat their slaves? "In the same way" as slaves are to serve their masters! Paul revolutionizes the whole of Roman society by presenting this new paradigm! Masters must respect and love slaves as Christ does. Only God has intrinsic authority. Masters only have delegated authority. What they are to do is to serve their Master in heaven. The best way to please our Master in heaven is to model servant leadership. Masters on earth play out their role in the drama of redemption by demonstrating what would Jesus do.

2. PROPHETIC ACT:By treating their slaves with love, kindness, and fairness, employers declare to angels, demons, and pre-believers—this is how our just God treats us! Employers are not to threaten their employees, but communicate the truth in love, for this is how Christ treats us. The word "kindness" in Greek is *chrestotes.* Early Christians saw the close connection with that word and Christ—*Christos.* We must show Christlikeness to all, no matter what our position in life may be.

3. GOD'S AUTHORITY STRUCTURE. Masters may be over their slaves and employers over their employees, but both must submit to the heavenly Master.

4. SERVANT SPIRIT. Masters must be slaves, too! They are love slaves of Jesus Christ. We must administrate God's way, so that God may be glorified! It has been said, that the ground beneath the cross is level. There is great equality in Christ. Paul said, "There is neither Jew nor Greek, slave nor free, male nor female, for you are all one in Christ Jesus" (Galatians 3:28). There is no favoritism with God.

5. REWARD AND ACCOUNTABILITY. One day every tongue will confess and every knee will bow before the Lord (Philippians 2:10-11). Jesus talked much about the judgment of God. We are accountable for what talents God has given us and the decisions we make.

Those who have been given much will be accountable for much. If we have been faithful over that which God has put under our charge, we shall be rewarded with greater responsibilities throughout eternity! This is a direct slap at Satan! He had much, being an archangel leading worship in heaven. But he rebelled, and will be condemned for all eternity.

Aquila and Priscilla impacted the marketplace (Acts 18: 1- 4). They were tentmakers, along with the Apostle Paul. They set the example of a powerful couple who served the Lord totally. They taught key leaders such as Apollos. They risked their lives to support and strengthen Paul. They stayed in certain cities to help establish the church. They used their home for a meeting place of the church. They were expendable for the cause of Christ. Paul said all the churches of the Gentiles are grateful to them (Romans 16:3-5). They set the standard for ministry in the marketplace.

II. CONSIDER ALL YOU DO AS HOLY

Biblically, Christians are set apart for God to influence the world. We are the salt of earth, the light of the world. We are to be priests unto God and a prophetic people touching our world for Christ. Unfortunately, only pastors and full-time workers were seen as a special class of people who served God wholeheartedly. The rest were "just laymen." Therefore, a major gap developed between the sacred and the secular which is not biblical. Instead of influencing the world, the church withdrew into itself. Yet throughout the Bible we see God's desires to thrust His people into the world.

The Apostle Paul was very sensitive to ministry in the marketplace. He saw it as the key to world evangelization. He himself was a tentmaker, as were Aquila and Priscilla. He undoubtedly made contacts and witnessed to other business people.

He spoke of those of "Caesar's household" implying the Gospel had touched the highest level of Roman society. He saw Lydia's influence in Philippi (Acts 16:14-15). She was a businesswoman who was a seller of purple. Her household was the first to come to Christ. The Gospel had its first inroad in Philippi with the conversion of Lydia and the women who were with her. Paul began to see the great power and influence of a Christian businesswoman.

Paul won a synagogue ruler (Sosthenes) and counted on his influence among Jewish people (Acts 18:17). Luke was a beloved physician who ministered to Paul and others. Philemon was a wealthy Christian who strategically used his house for the Gospel (Philemon 1:1) Zenas, the lawyer, was needed by Paul (Titus 3:13).

In Romans 16 Paul mentions by name twenty-six key people in Rome, most of whom were not in "full-time ministry." Many were outstanding Christians who had made their mark in both the church and the marketplace. These were strategic leaders Paul would likely work with when he actually came to Rome. Indeed, he saw the whole body of Christ doing the work of the ministry (Ephesians 4:11-13). Our lives are to be a spiritual act of worship to God (Romans 12:1). We worship God in everything that we do. We live out the drama of redemption in all our activities. We must see each vocation as part of God's holy calling. What potential when you see your life this way! May God call many of you to the marketplace to affect people's lives!

III. PREPARE TO SERVE THE LORD!

We used to teach that there was one vocation for each person. Find it and you find God's will. But our world is far more complex than that. A hundred years ago, career choices were few—butcher, baker, candlestick maker, doctor, lawyer, teacher, etc. Now we are spoilt for choices. There are easily over 100,000 career choices! No wonder many young people are confused about their future! Beyond that, most of you will have between three to ten different careers in your lifetime. But far more critical than all these changes is that this teaching of one vocation per person put the focus on the wrong areas. It did not prepare us to be a witness, to minister in the marketplace, or to adjust to the changes in our lives. We need to take another look at our vocations from a biblical base.

PURPOSE: "You have created all things and for your pleasure they are and were created" (Revelation 4:11). God created us to serve Him. We are an expression of God, an epistle of Christ to others.

PREPARATION. Develop the total man: spiritually, intellectually, emotionally, and socially. Be all you can be for Christ! Moses spent forty years in Egypt and forty years in desert in preparation before God used him in the great work of leading the people out of Egypt. And remember, half of the New Testament was written by a highly-educated Paul who allowed God to transform his life. Preparation is vital so that we can share what God has given us.

Because most people will be involved in three to ten careers in a lifetime, God's will involves development in many areas of our personality and skills. I tell young people to develop as broad a foundation as possible so they can see where many of their talents lie and specialize later on. To be an effective witness, EQ (emotional quotient)—how we relate to people, has become increasingly important. Because we must adjust to new organizational cultures and vocations, we must learn to be adaptable and flexible. If we are stuck on one way of doing things, we will not be open to what is needed for the future. Then we will not impact our world for Christ.

PROCLAMATION. If you go to a university or a new place of work, remember to make this your place of witness immediately. It is easier to begin right and let others know of your faith early. Then people can watch your life. Of course one must be very careful where witnessing for Christ is a very sensitive matter.

PLANNING. Good stewardship demands that we must be wise in time management, money management, and values. To the believer, time is more sacred than gold. Paul says, "redeem the time", or "buy up the time." Literally the word "redeem" means to buy up out of the marketplace (Ephesians 5:16, KJV).

There is a Chinese proverb that says, "An inch of time, an inch of gold. An inch of gold cannot buy an inch of time." The NIV says "making the most of every opportunity..." Financially, also, we must be good stewards. Of course, Christians live by faith in every area, but it is equally important that we plan for adverse unforeseen circumstances that require our personal financial reserves. If we continually live on the edge of our financial means, we will be in a difficult situation when we face job transition. We need to be wise and cautious in whatever areas of investment we get into. Money is to be used for the glory of God. We must be sure that we are building on biblical values where the solid rock is Christ Jesus. Whatever is not built upon firm foundations will not stand.

Seeking God's will for marketplace ministry means understanding our biblical roles as priest and prophet, learning how to relate to people, being flexible, and keeping a self discipline that will help us not to panic in the transition times.

IV. LEARN TO MAKE GODLY DECISIONS

Set priorities to glorify God over your lifetime. You can make a difference in people's lives! When I come to a major decision, I find it helpful to write down the pros and cons of all the choices. What will best glorify God? This sets everything in proper perspective.

Then, I pray about one alternative at a time. If you have three good alternatives and tried to pray about all three, you would easily become confused. Pray about one alternative first. God will either give you assurance about that alternative or doubts will seem to dominate. If doubts dominate, move on to pray concerning the second alternative. When God gives you the assurance of His desire, move ahead by faith on that alternative and set aside the other possibilities.

Take Isaiah 30:21 as your own promise from God: "Whether you turn to the right or to the left, your ears will hear a voice behind you saying, "This is the way; walk in it."

If none of the alternatives receives God's "go" sign, continue actively where you are and wait for God's further word. Another alternative may be apparent only a little later. Talk to a mature Spirit-filled Christian friend in whom you can confide. This is especially valuable if that friend also sees his calling in the marketplace. He will be able to counsel and pray with you.

It makes a difference to know someone else shares your problems and desires to do God's will just like you do. You will gain new insights on what God wants you to do. Don't just take anyone's advice. Go to well-informed, spiritually mature Christians. Accurate information is better than rumors or hearsay!

Often God allows you to make the choice by faith. This involves your maturity, your capacity to assume responsibility, and your decisions as to how to glorify God most effectively. Don't wait for lightning to strike. God will always honor your faith. You may not always have an easy path after making your decision, but you will develop in Christlikeness, and your steps of faith will help you to touch people for Christ.

In retrospect, God does speak directly to some Christians concerning going into a certain field of work. The key is your willingness to respond. Do you have a great passion for that work? Do you have the abilities that are needed?

In my own experience, the Lord began laying a message upon my heart before I ever preached a sermon. For a whole year those thoughts seemingly burned within me, until I had to say with Paul, "Woe is unto me, if I preach not the Gospel!" (1 Corinthians 9:16) Then God opened the door of opportunity for me to share. Since that first sermon as a teenager, God has miraculously opened doors of ministry for me.

God does not want to leave us in confusion about His plan for our lives. I can unhesitatingly say that I have been in the will of God in all my life as a Christian. I've never doubted it. That does not mean I have never made mistakes or I was right all the time. But I expect God to lead. I know I am in His hands. I read His Word and listen as He speaks. How can I know the leading of the Spirit? It all depends upon sensitivity and the Word of God.

If the Holy Spirit leads us to do something, it will always be in harmony with the teachings of the Word of God. That's why I say: Read the Word. Know what it says. Begin listening to the impressions God makes upon your heart in your prayer time. Watch for God-given opportunities and take advantage of them.

God has given you talents and interests. Don't bury them! Develop them for His glory! Talk to your pastor or a mature Christian friend. Then, "Commit your way unto the Lord, trust in Him, and He will do this" (Psalms 37:5).

I wish to commission all of you to minister into the marketplace. It is as sacred a calling as mine is to preach from the pulpit. Start thinking about your vocation as your place of ministry. You'll be surprised how God can use you where you are.

CHAPTER 12

INTEGRITY EMPOWERS YOUR ROLE!

Staying Power, Reputational Power, Organizational Power, Spiritual Power

Matthew 25:14-30, Proverbs 22:1

In the parable of the talents Jesus talks about three servants. Each one is entrusted with a certain amount of money. They were told exactly the same thing by the Master. Two are rewarded because they were good and faithful servants. They did what they were supposed to do with that money and pleased the Master equally because they were faithful to their task. It was not an issue of who had more ability.

On the contrary, the third servant failed to carry out his duties in investing the funds. He found excuses for his lack of faithfulness. By doing nothing he had violated his master's trust. He lacked integrity. The master judged him for it and declared, "For everyone who has will be given more, and he will have an abundance. Whoever does not have, even what he has will be taken from him" (Matthew 25:29). Those who operate from a basis of integrity will be blessed by God. Integrity empowers us to fulfill our potential for God's glory. We are to be good and faithful servants of all that God has entrusted to us.

In one major city in Canada during the 1970s, Christian business people were seen as one of the highest risk groups. This was because some had mishandled their finances, got involved in financial scams, and tried to overprice the real estate market because of their desire for prosperity—the big word in Christian circles in those days.

Recently, someone in our church was a victim of unscrupulous business practices. She was told that she too could play the game, and get rich! She suffered badly because of it. Now, she is determined to live in integrity and glorify God, no matter what. Again recently, gigantic corporations like Enron and WorldCom literally deceived millions of people and defrauded them of their livelihoods. Some of these CEOs even claimed to be Christians!

Major surveys among *Fortune 500* business leaders indicate the key quality they look for in leaders is integrity. In one Third World country a church leader said to me, "If only we could have a semblance of integrity, we would be a lot better off." He was deploring the sad state of affairs to which some pastors had fallen into.

Many highly gifted people have seen their lives, families, and businesses fall apart because they lacked the big "I" word: Integrity. Someone once said, "Integrity is what you are when no one is watching you." Richard Dortch was a most outstanding Christian leader and a vice president of the PTL television network that fell in a major scandal. He confesses that he succumbed to temptation and lost his integrity. Read his major work, *Integrity, How I Lost It and My Journey Back* (Green Forest, Arkansas: New Leaf Press, 1991). Now he is invited to give a yearly lecture at Harvard on the subject of integrity.

Usually integrity hinges on three lifestyle issues: money, sex, and power. I would like to talk more about these three areas before continuing on about the incredible power of integrity. Jesus tells us if we are faithful with a few things, He will put us in charge of many things (Matthew 25:23).

Watch how a person handles his own life and the small decisions and you will see how he handles the bigger issues.

I. Integrity of Lifestyle

Money

First, I believe in tithing to God. Whatever I do, I want to be honorable in my relationship to God because He is the one I am most accountable to. That sets the standard for how I face other issues. My wife and I discuss our mutual usage of finances. We are open with each other. We never question each other for smaller purchases like books, gifts, and clothing. But we are accountable to each other in major gifts and purchases and our overall budget.

Specifically, I am accountable to my family, the pastoral and administrative team, the executive church board, and to my congregation. If I work within these lines of accountability, I can serve under a huge umbrella that will cover my reputation in ministry.

If I am a man of integrity, this sets the example for the pastoral team and board. Together we serve as a covering for the entire church.

Everyone should be able to see what kind of church we have through our service to the Lord. They will give financially to support the church and her missionary vision. They will serve faithfully in ministries.

Because the leadership puts the kingdom of God and the church first, the members can freely minister and put God first in their lives. Leadership must be above reproach or criticism when it comes to policy decisions and handling of finances.

SEX

This is a perennial problem area. There are several reasons for this. People can now privately access pornographic material on the internet. They do not realize how easily they can become addicted to cybersex. Because of frequent overseas travels, some fall into temptation. They think they are no longer accountable to anyone, since they are anonymous in the new location. Often people underestimate their weaknesses in this area. They think they are strong to resist temptations, but they are unaware of their vulnerabilities, loneliness, and frustrations, or unable to handle their own sexuality properly.

To overcome these temptations, we need a balanced lifestyle and people to whom we are regularly accountable to. I constantly remind myself that greater men than I am have fallen and ruined their reputations and ministries. When the pornographic icons pop up on my computer I tell people in the office so I can be accountable to them and I delete the icons immediately.

When I travel without my family, I am aware of my feelings and loneliness. I am conscious that the devil may exploit those times to tempt me. So, I call my wife every day to catch up with her. I take time to seek God and to renew His calling upon my life. I seek to develop a lifestyle of healthy friendships with both male and female to keep my perspective in balance. When I was a teenager my pastor suggested reading the book of Proverbs regularly because it warns us about the traps of sexual promiscuity. I seek not to overtire myself or overstress myself. The devil tempts us most at these times.

We need to seriously count the cost of becoming addicted in this area and realize its devastation to our Christian witness. Ministries have been ruined, families have been broken and reputations have been destroyed because of failure in this area.

Power

We all possess power to varying degrees. And how we use that power can tell a lot about who we are. Someone once said, "Power corrupts, and absolute power corrupts absolutely." Of course that is a generalization. God has absolute power and yet He is not corruptible. But all too often the quote is true.

When people assume power over anything (e.g., a person, family, finances, position in an organization), there are huge temptations to misuse and abuse that power. The list of dictators who abused their power is endless. Examples are: Stalin, Lenin, Mussolini, Hitler, Caeceasceau, Idi Amin, Saddam Hussein.

As Christians, we must be sure that we do all things with the right attitudes. We are here to glorify God, i.e. we do our best for whatever organization we are working for. As good stewards of all that God has given us, we have no other choice. We should be known for our diligence, conscientiousness, and honesty.

We should not seek to sabotage the organization or spread gossip to hurt another person. This is both true in the corporate sector and within the church. Gossip only becomes bigger and bigger and can ruin a person's reputation or life. As a result, it may also hurt the kingdom of God.

Of course, if there is sin, it must be confronted. But I have always tried to protect the church or mission organization I have worked with. The cause of God's kingdom is greater than any personal hurts or injustices I may have felt. I have never regretted that decision. When I entrust my future to God, God takes care of me. And God will judge those who are unjust.

If we are executives or CEOs, we must think of what is the best for all concerned: the stakeholders, the employees, and the corporate culture. When we conscientiously work at proper decision-making, people will respect that process. They will know we seek to maximize the potential of the business for the glory of God and the welfare of all concerned. If greed and selfishness had not entered the picture, organizations like Enron would never have devastated the lives of so many thousands of people.

Dr. Archibald Hart is a world-renowned Christian psychologist. He points out that many "successful" CEOs fall into a vicious cycle of four "As".

Success drives them to *Arrogance*, thinking they are naturally great and success came their way because of their ingenuity. Next, they move on to *Aloneness*, where they are no longer accountable to other people but make decisions independently, regardless of advisability or ethics of the situation. Then, the thrill of *Adventure* becomes addictive, where they venture into things never tried before and move into the area of the questionable. Finally, they fall into *Adultery*. (From Dr. Hart's address at an Eagle's Conference in Singapore, August 22, 2003). Why have we seen so much failure in leaders? It began with arrogance. Proverbs 16:18 says, "Pride goes before destruction, a haughty spirit before a fall."

Power is best seen in the light of Christ's second coming. He alone has all power. Power is not meant for temporary or personal gain. We are to be faithful stewards of all we have. We are to commit everything to Christ in the light of His coming. God is the ultimate Judge who will judge all our works, our attitudes, and behaviors. He sees who we are in secret. He has set the standards in the Scripture. We cannot escape from them.

II. Power in Integrity

Staying Power

There is staying power in integrity. I have shared openly and freely with my congregation concerning the crosses I have had to bear in my life. I think I have been crucified at least five times in my ministry! My openness in sharing is to show others how they can be victorious too.

What kept me strong and faithful even when misunderstood? Or when people accused me of lacking integrity? Or when I was unfairly treated? It was in knowing that I am living my life for God's glory. I was being true to God and to myself. That has kept me marching forward for 42 consecutive years of full-time ministry. And I am still excited about serving Jesus. I am still growing in my preaching ministry. I am learning more of God's wonderful and mysterious ways of doing things.

Other Christian leaders may have given up long ago because of discouragement or criticism or because circumstances that did not turn out well. If they only knew that God is their judge. That He alone would justify us and turn every event around for his own glory! I like what Charles Spurgeon taught his ministerial students. He said they did not need to defend themselves when criticized. If they were living for God, God would be their defense and the criticisms would roll off like snowballs.

When you know you are doing your best according to godly values, you have inner strength that keeps you going even when problems arise or when you are wronged by others. You know that you are seeking to please God alone. God will take care of you. You will dare to face any amount of pain, because you are not living for man's favor, but to fulfill God's plan for your life. This is why Paul could "press on to the goal to win the prize for which God has called me heavenward in Christ Jesus" (Philippians 3:14). Nothing could stop such a man.

I think of the pioneer and founder of Grace Assembly in Singapore. Pastor Lula Baird has simply been unstoppable. Regardless of her strengths or weaknesses, or how people treated her or how her health failed her, she has been an inspiration to all. At the age of 99 she is still vibrantly testifying for Jesus Christ!

Many good things can happen if we stay in a situation long enough for God to change the circumstances. I have discovered that so many things can change if we give God a chance to do it in His time. Let me tell you the story of Aggie Hurst.

The Hurst family is well known in the Assemblies of God worldwide. Aggie's parents went to Africa to try to win the Africans for Jesus. Due to the scarcity of good medical care, her mother died when a disease broke out in an African village. Aggie's father felt disillusioned. He gave his baby daughter, Aggie, to an American couple. So, Aggie grew up in America, attended Bible College, and went on to become a great missionary in her own right. Aggie's father, on the other hand, feeling defeated, went back to Europe. He became an alcoholic and would move from one cheap hotel to another.

One year, Aggie went to a conference of pastors in Africa, where her father had started his "failed ministry" years before. An African pastor looked at her, recognized the resemblance and asked, "Are you Aggie Hurst?" She replied "Yes". He jumped up and down, danced, and then hugged her. Then, he continued, "Years ago your father came to Africa and won me to the Lord. He left, thinking he had sacrificed much for no results. But I became a preacher. Now, in this very area are hundreds of thousands of Christians because of the work your father began!" Aggie's father had not failed. God is the Lord of the harvest. He should have stayed on to see how God would turn the situation around.

If we do move on to another job or ministry, however, we don't have to carry the baggage of hurts with us if we have served with integrity. Too often we try to justify ourselves before our fellow man. I remember well hearing someone tell me, "David, you are not a leader!" I did not reply because I knew God's calling upon my life. Though the statement hurt me, I knew the gifts God had given me. Because I knew I had done my best for God's glory, I could have effective closure of one phase of my life and move on wholeheartedly to the next. Now, nobody would say to me, "David, you are not a leader!" I certainly make many mistakes of judgment and I dare not boast of any special leadership skills, but God has graciously allowed me to pastor a very exciting church.

Satan tempts us in the area of condemnation. If we profess one thing outwardly but are inconsistent inwardly, then Satan labels us "hypocrites". That is where a lack of integrity will cause us to break down. If we are really living like the devil, pretending to be spiritual or righteous, then we have no inner strength to help us.

F. F. Bruce wrote *Paul the Apostle of the Heart Set Free*, (Grand Rapids: Eerdmans, 1977). In the title page, Bruce quotes 2 Corinthians 3:17 (Basic English Version), "Where the Spirit of the Lord is, the heart is free." Paul was a free man. He was not held captive by other people's opinions of him, by persecution, or by past failures. He was free to be led by the Spirit of God, to change the world for Christ. Your heart cannot be set free if it condemns you continually. That is why Paul says, "There is now no condemnation for those who are in Christ Jesus" (Romans 8:1). Of course, no one is perfect. We do need to receive God's forgiveness, and to forgive ourselves for our imperfections. As we grow towards maturity, we should not expect perfection. If our talk and our walk are consistent, we can have staying power to carry on. People with integrity can run the race well and will have the strength to finish it.

REPUTATIONAL POWER

Integrity is important to establishing a good name. In Proverbs 22:1 we read, "A good name is more desirable than great riches; to be esteemed is better than silver or gold." A man's reputation is critical to his effectiveness. This is not the same as seeking fame. Fame is having a good name for our own sake.

As Christians, we represent Christ in all that we do. God entrusts his reputation to us! We must preserve our good name at all costs so that Christ may be glorified.

When others know you will not compromise, that you will stand by what you say, they know you are trustworthy. You are a person other people dare to follow. You walk the walk as well as talk the talk. Others may laugh at your commitment to God but deep inside they will know you are worthy of respect.

With a good reputation people will not only buy your product, but they will also find your testimony credible. When you are down, you will be able to rise again. But with a bad reputation, no one will be around to try to help out. No one will be able to trust you or to respect you.

I am saddened by top leaders who have lived so powerfully for God most of their lives and then they make one tragic mistake. They mishandle funds, they are seduced by power or they are tempted by immorality. A Chinese proverb says, "One misstep leads to a thousand agonies." Suddenly, all they accomplished is diminished by that one wrong move. They lose their reputation, their family, their position, their ministry, their effectiveness.

Proverbs 16:18 tells us that "Pride goes before destruction, a haughty spirit before a fall." We must never think we have arrived. It was when King David thought he had achieved much that he stayed home during a time of war. In 2 Samuel 1-10 he was climbing uphill and making great progress in serving the Lord. Then he committed adultery with Bathsheba. Then it was downhill all the way as detailed in 2 Samuel 11-24.

We will all make mistakes, but people will forgive us more readily if we have integrity. They will know that we did not hurt people or cause pain in a situation intentionally. They will give us the benefit of the doubt, rather than read us suspiciously.

Organizational Power

When a family, a business, or an institution operates with integrity, people are willing to work harder, sacrifice more, and become more loyal to its goals and directions. They will realize no one is being taken advantage of. They will seek to provide covering for each other and encourage each other. They know that the operating principles are based on integrity rather than sneaky or devious ways.

That is why I mentioned earlier that the number one trait those *Fortune 500* executives look for in a leader is integrity. They know such a leader will be fair to all and increase the motivation in a company. In addition, other organizations like to deal with companies that are known for their integrity. They know they will not be shortchanged.

If we are executives or CEO's, we must think of what is best for all concerned: the stakeholders, the employees, and the corporate culture. When we conscientiously work at proper decision-making, people will respect that process. They will know we seek to maximize the potential of the business for the glory of God and the welfare of all concerned.

When you do things God's way, then God will bless you abundantly. This is not to say you will always be successful in financial terms. Sometimes it may even seem that the wicked may prosper (Psalm 73:3). Many in the business world feel they must use corrupt methodology to gain the upper hand. They feel they must "play the game" in a certain way. This type of success is temporary. But if you choose to put God first, then God can pour out His blessings upon such a venture. And God's blessings are true blessings that are lasting. Proverbs 16:8 says, "Better a little with righteousness than much gain with injustice." Then God can bless you with true, abundant, biblical prosperity.

A church will grow best if people know it is operated on the highest principles. If people question the way finances are handled or the way they are being treated, it makes the task of growing a church all the more difficult. If money, sex, or power becomes an issue, then that church is in dire straits. God is honored when any organization is operating with integrity.

A family will grow best when children see their parents living a lifestyle of integrity before God. That provides a covering of protection for the children, so they don't have to suffer the pain of a broken home or face confusion from parents living double lives. When children can look at their parents and know that they are godly, they are truly blessed their entire lives! What a gift we can give our children!

God honors those who honor him. If we truly honor God, then any benefits truly become our possessions because these are given from God. Any ill-gotten gain or gain from our cleverness can be taken away. But when we do things God's way, God blesses us.

Matthew 6:33, "But seek first His kingdom and His righteousness, and all these things will be given to you as well."

Spiritual Power

James 5:16 says "The prayer of a righteous man is powerful and effective." God has given so much work for us to do in His kingdom. This verse tells us that a righteous lifestyle results in power from God! The context of this verse is about praying for the sick, forgiving sins, and praying for miracles as Elijah did.

Note James' emphasis here. He is not saying "If we have the gift of healings or miracles, we shall see power with God." That may be true too. But he is saying that if we are consistent in serving the Lord, we shall see more than our share! We will have great confidence before God. We will not burn out before our time, or commit some tragic sin that shortens our effective service for God. If we remain true to God, we will discover that God remains true to His Word and to us. We will see mighty things happen in the kingdom of God.

Jesus said, "Blessed are the pure in heart, for they will see God" (Matthew 5:8). If we believe God is fully in charge of our lives, then no obstacle can deter us from His greater plan for us. We know that the will of God shall be accomplished in His time, and in His way. God's will for you is part of God's kingdom and plan for all mankind. His will be done! We are simply His servants!

I have discovered that in Christ every detour leads to divine destiny; every crucifixion leads to resurrection life; and every despair results in delight. That has been the story of my life. When I feel discouraged and I cannot go on any further, I plod on still. My integrity involves God's call upon my life. I have to be true to that. All else may fail, but my reason for existence is to walk in God's will. And when I keep walking, I see His glory, His strength, and His plan. If we can see God in the darkest hour of our situation, then we have hope. If we truly look to Him as our only source of supply, then we shall see how He supplies miraculously. There is power in knowing "This is my Father's world!" Despite the evil in this world, the unfairness around and the devil's cunning deception, God is in control!

Someone at Grace Assembly gave me the greatest compliment I think I shall ever receive. He said, "Pastor Lim, you lead by your integrity. It is very apparent." I am humbled by that. What an awesome responsibility! All the more I must continue to examine myself in the areas of money, sex, and power. I must realize the awesome power of integrity: its staying power, reputational power, organizational power, and spiritual power. I must not take for granted that everyone will think this way about me. Integrity is between God and me.

If I lose my integrity, I have lost it all. I may run the race well for most of the journey and still blow it on the last lap. I pray that I shall be able to say with the Apostle Paul, "I have fought the good fight, I have finished the race, I have kept the faith" (2 Timothy 4:7).

God's will for your life is one that is built upon integrity. My challenge to Christians today: If we let our light shine brightly, people will see and know the reality of our power with God. And we can move ahead with the toughest challenges, knowing that God's blessings are upon us!

CHAPTER 13

GLORIFY GOD IN THE COSMOS!

Walking Through Ephesians

God is preparing a people anointed by the Spirit to accomplish mighty things! In the Old Testament the people of God disobeyed and broke God's covenant. Now, in New Testament times, God is fulfilling His plan through a people of power and praise.

Normally, the first two thirds of Paul's epistles are doctrinal teaching followed by teaching on practical living in the final third. Romans is a good example of this. Romans 1-11 lays the theological basis for justification by faith in Christ. Romans 12-16 show us how to live out this faith. But Ephesians is different. Even though Paul is bound in a Roman prison and though the churches of Ephesus and Asia Minor face many problems, Paul writes with a freedom and a perspective that transcends all these problems. Ephesians 1-3 focus on worship, Ephesians 4:1-6:9 discuss our walk, and Ephesians 6:10-19 teaches us about warfare. Let us survey some of the key thrusts of Ephesians.

EPHESIANS 1
GIVE GOD ALL THE GLORY!

God's glory is the theme of all of scripture. The kingdom of God will defeat Satan's kingdom. Chapter One begins with a hymn of praise with three stanzas. Ephesians 1:3-14 is actually one long sentence without a main verb expressed in the Greek! When the Apostle Paul is worshipping God he is not concerned about perfect grammar! The first stanza praises God the Father, the second stanza praises Christ the Son, and the third stanza praises the Holy Spirit. Each stanza ends with "to the praise of His glory." Everything that is done in the drama of redemption is for the glory of God.

Before my wife and I came to Grace Assembly in Singapore we were in the mountains of Baguio City, Philippines at the Asia Pacific Theological Seminary. I had accepted the call from the church to be their pastor. But in the months before we were to arrive in Singapore, I prayed in earnest. "God, what is it that you want us to do in Singapore?" God's simple reply was, "Give God all the glory."

As one who taught biblical studies and church growth, I thought I knew that lesson. God deserves all the glory for any accomplishments and successes. Even when people might compliment us on a sermon preached, we were to give glory to God. But it seemed like too simple an answer, so I continued praying, seeking God for what He wanted to do through our ministry in Singapore.

Day after day, God gave the same reply: "Give God all the glory." Then it dawned on me that perhaps God wanted me to press on in prayer for a deeper insight from Him. So I prayed, "God, I need more. Give me more!" God's reply startled me. "David, you want more, I'll give you more. Give God the glory, or else your ministry is finished!" That statement shook me. It revolutionized my life more than all the seminars I have attended and all the years of biblical studies I had taken. It was profound.

In fact, glorifying God is the heart of the drama of redemption. We declare God has won, and Satan has lost! It is no wonder God's command in the Ten Commandments to "not make yourself an idol ..." contains the phrase, "I, the Lord your God, am a jealous God..."

We are to have no other gods before Him (1st commandment). We are not to make any idols (2nd commandment). We are not to misuse the name of the Lord our God (3rd commandment). We are to keep a Sabbath day holy before the Lord (4th commandment). God must be first and foremost in our lives!

God is jealous for His name and His glory, but not in a selfish way. When we give God all the glory, He may then pour out His glory upon us. No wonder the Lord's Prayer begins with "Our Father in heaven, hallowed be your name, your kingdom come, your will be done on earth as it is in heaven (Matthew 6:9-10)." We are to revere His name, and desire His kingdom and will. From Genesis to Revelation, the glory of God and the kingdom of God is the key issue.

It changed my philosophy. I was not merely a fully dedicated servant of God seeking to train leadership and reaching those without Christ. I was now lifted to the heavenly realms in Christ Jesus, as co-partner with Him in the greatest plan of all creation! He has a plan. It shall be accomplished! My role was simply to glorify Him with my whole being, to play my part in the drama of redemption. I was not here to impress people, but to be faithful to God alone.

It changed my methodology. I could be far more patient, knowing God was in control of all things. God placed me as senior pastor over Grace Assembly. Whether I met opposition or support, I must remain as the covering for the church and not let the enemy attack and hurt her. When I came against problems, I discovered there are always three perspectives: my view, the other person's view, and God's view. God's view transcends all other views. It changed the way I relate to people. I know that not everyone will love me. In fact, there may be those who suspect my motives. But, to give God the glory, I must keep on loving them and treat them as valuable members of the body of Christ. I am not here to make everyone into my own image, but to develop everyone into the image of Christ.

It changed my preaching and approach to worship. We come before the audience of Almighty God. My preaching is not meant to impress people with my abilities (though I am fully aware of the importance of effective communication), but I must preach so that God will receive all glory and our people will draw closer to God.

I understand that what I do on the stage of the drama of redemption will impact the cosmos. The angels will rejoice and the demons will be chased away, when I minister God's way. When we worship as a congregation, we do not have to compare ourselves with other congregations. We may not come up to their "professional" standards. But our hearts must be pure, our motive must be simple, our method must bring high praise to God, and we must realize that we are on holy ground.

When we as a congregation offer worship that is pleasing to God, the angels rejoice with us, the demons flee away, and we are declaring that God's kingdom shall prevail for all eternity. All will recognize that our church genuinely worships the living God.

It changed my approach to missions. Now our task is to declare God's glory over the nations! It started with me personally giving the glory to God. Then the church learned how to glorify God in unity and purity and worship. Then we have a mandate to declare His glory to those who have not heard the gospel. Prayer must under gird all that we do in missions. Unselfishness and not seeking to make a name for ourselves was important. We must not lord it over the national leaders of other countries, but since they are equally vital members in the work of God, we must work in partnership with them, seeking to bless them and step by step release authority to them to take over their own churches. One amazing result of this approach is that over the past 5 years alone we have started 505 thriving and growing churches averaging over 25,000 in weekly attendance in many countries of Asia.

It changed my view of success and failure. It is not a matter of whether I was right and others were wrong. Decisions have not all gone my way. Ministry must not exalt me, but must exalt God alone. When our English congregation tripled and the Chinese side grew by 90%, I realized it was not because of me, but because of the mighty gracious hand of our sovereign Lord.

When I made mistakes I would have to commit them to God. He was the Lord over my mistakes, too! He could turn around every mistake for His glory. I would not need to dwell on my wrong decisions or actions. For the benefit and encouragement of pastors reading this, believe me, I've made more than my share of wrong decisions! What a liberating truth!

When you give God all the glory, He watches over every decision you make and turns it for His glory! To pastor a large multi-cultural church with four generations of people is no easy matter! It stretches me beyond my limits. But then I realize God is in charge of this church!

I discovered that the theme of the whole Bible is the glory of God vanquishing the works of Satan. I discovered that the theme of the drama of redemption is "God has won, and Satan has lost."

When we do things God's way, the wisdom of God is shown to all the principalities and powers. If we do not react when unfairly treated or misunderstood, then God wins the battle and Satan loses. When we rise above our discouragements and claim God's kingdom first and foremost, we win, too. Even though others may feel we are defeated, we never lose when we do things God's way. Though circumstances may look glum, we have victory because Christ has overcome the world. The Westminster Catechism says, "The chief end of man is to glorify God and enjoy Him forever."

If I valued my ministry and calling, I must give God all the glory—or else my ministry was finished! So many leaders leave their ministries bitter. Some even destroy their ministries, churches are split, and terrible disunity arises among God's people, because some are more intent on defending personal rights and personal glory than on the glory of God.

Paul first praises the Father who chose us in Christ before the foundations of the world. Some say, because God created us, man must have a special purpose in this world. But even before God created the world He had a plan for us and set us apart for His holy purpose. He prepared to bless us with every blessing in the heavenly realms. The purpose? To the praise of His glorious grace (Ephesians 1:3-6).

Then Paul praises the Son for the redemption plan, for forgiveness, for lavishing wisdom and understanding concerning God's great plan that will be put into effect "when the times have reached their fulfillment." We were chosen, predestined and blessed to be "for the praise of His glory" (Ephesians 1:7-12).

In the third stanza of the song, Paul includes the Gentiles. He reveals a sense of humor with his interplay of "we" and "you" in this song. In the first two stanzas he uses "we." "We" refers to Jews. Paul teases the Gentiles that the blessings were first of all for Jews. Then, finally in v13 he says, "and you also were included in Christ..." referring to the Gentiles! When my daughters were young children, I loved to tease them at dinner time. When my wife made a tasty soup or a special favorite dish, I would say "All mine! This is all for me!" My daughters knew that, as their father, I always wanted the best for them. They would simply reply, "Oh, dad, stop teasing us!"

In the same way, Paul says the blessings of God were first of all for the Jews. Then, in the mercy and grace of God, the Gentiles were included in all the blessings! We Gentiles should be all the more grateful for God's grace. Our Heavenly Father will not deprive us of any good thing.

Paul then says, "Having believed, you were marked in Him with a seal, the promised Holy Spirit"(Ephesians 1:13). While some scholars would say the "seal" represents an inner witness or conviction in our hearts, it is important to note that the word "seal" as used in Scripture is always an outward sign.

"...the sealing with the Spirit has a specific beginning but it still continues. It enables the saints to do things they would not do of their own resources; to participate in the praise of God's glory (1:6, 12, 14); to make known God's wisdom to the powers (3:10); to carry abroad the news of peace (6:15); to wield the sword of the Spirit which is the word of God (6:17)."

Such sealing by the Spirit is much more than assurance of personal salvation, and more precious than individual peace of mind. It makes God's chosen men troubadours before God for the joy of the whole world. ... Those sealed are an exhibition of God's love and power. Theirs is a mission." (Markus Barth, *Ephesians 1-3, Vol. 34*, Garden City, N.Y.: Doubleday and Company, 1974, p. 141.)

In fact, this verse parallels Paul's question to the Ephesians in Acts 19:2, "Did you receive the Holy Spirit when you believed?"

In Acts 19:6 Luke records this reception of the Holy Spirit: "When Paul placed his hands on them, the Holy Spirit came on them, and they spoke in tongues and prophesied." This is not to say that we do not have the Holy Spirit at salvation. The disciples had seen the risen Christ and had believed. Jesus had breathed the Holy Spirit upon them (John 20:22). But Jesus still wanted them to receive another experience in the Holy Spirit.

Barth says, "According to the book of Acts such authentication (of Gentile converts) takes place and is recognized when Jews or Gentiles begin to praise God and his mighty deeds in the astonishing form of 'speaking in tongues.' (Barth, Ibid., p. 140)."

There are two ways to understand the phrase, "the promised Holy Spirit." The first way is that the Holy Spirit was promised to Jesus' disciples. John the Baptist had prophesied that "I baptize you with water for repentance. But ... He will baptize you with the Holy Spirit and with fire." Jesus promised the outpouring of the Holy Spirit on the Day of Pentecost.

In Luke 24:49 Jesus told his disciples to "stay in the city until you have been clothed with power from on high." In Acts 1:8 Jesus promised his disciples would "receive power when the Holy Spirit comes upon you; and you will be my witnesses in Jerusalem, and in all Judea and Samaria, and to the ends of the earth." From this view, the promised Holy Spirit would empower Jesus' disciples for service.

The second way to understand "promised Holy Spirit" is "Holy Spirit of promise." In the Greek, this is a perfectly good reading of the passage. Then, the Holy Spirit brings with Him all the promises of God and the gifts of the Spirit.

Interestingly, in Matthew 7:11 Jesus says, "If you, then, though you are evil, know how to give good gifts to your children, how much more will your Father in heaven give good gifts to those who ask him!" In Luke 11:13, Jesus says, "How much more will your Father in heaven give the Holy Spirit to those who ask him!" The Matthew account says the Father gives gifts. The Luke account says the Father gives the Holy Spirit. There is no contradiction. What is better than receiving a good gift? It is receiving the Holy Spirit who brings all the gifts!

This flows right into Ephesians 1:14 "who is a deposit guaranteeing our inheritance until the redemption of those who are God's possession--to the praise of his glory."

The Holy Spirit brings the rest of the blessings of God to us. It is as if we put a down payment on a piece of property. This is a guarantee that we intend to pay the rest of the price. The gift of the Holy Spirit is just the down payment!

The Holy Spirit has come to fulfill all that God promises for our lives! He keeps us and leads us until Jesus returns for His church! All this is to the praise and glory of God. So everything the Trinity does on our behalf reflects back to give full glory to God. Everything we do should also give all the glory to God. This is the underlying theme of all of scripture and of the drama of redemption.

Ephesians 2-3
Christ Overcame Every Hurdle

In Ephesians 2 and 3 Paul tells us no hurdle is too high. Jesus Christ broke down every barrier between Jew and Gentile so they could be one in Christ! There was a huge gap, spiritually, culturally, and socially between Jews and Gentiles.

The Jews were proud of being God's chosen people, of having received Moses' Law, of having the Davidic throne which was to last forever, and of being the recipients of the promises of God. They saw the Gentiles as foreigners to the covenants of the promise, aliens, strangers, without hope and without God in this world (Ephesians 2:12, 19). Jews thought the Gentiles were unclean for eating pork (most Chinese would then be considered unclean! Their love of pork is well-known) and not being circumcised. The Gentiles, on the other hand, thought the Jews were weird, narrow, and disconnected from the rest of the world.

The gap between Jew and Gentile was as great as the differences between man and woman! When I first married my darling wife, May, I did not realize the huge differences! Sometimes she would say something and then say "Forget it." As a man, I took that literally, and forgot it! Since then, I have learned, when a woman says "Forget it", you had better not forget it!

I have learned that men are more left-brained thinkers (objectivity and logic-oriented) as opposed to being right-brained thinkers (emotional, intuitive and aesthetic). Men love to discuss sports, world news, politics or business. Women, on the other hand, think with both sides of the brain. They think more holistically. A woman can multi-task. She can cook dinner, care for children, discuss business on the phone and read a newspaper, all at the same time! That confuses the man! He does not know whether she is speaking out of the right side of the brain or the left! When women talk with each other, they are often intimate, looking into each other's eyes and holding hands. When men talk to other men usually they look in opposite directions and only occasionally look at the other to be sure he is still there! And if God could bridge the gap between Jew and Gentile, He can also bridge the gap between male and female! Every obstacle can be overcome!

The early church faced major problems that could have easily destroyed the church. Look at the following problems the book of Acts records: persecution (Acts 4), deceit (5), apparent discrimination between Hebrew Jewish widows and Greek Jewish widows (6), martyrdom (7), the occult and racial discrimination (8), Saul's persecution (9), the Gentile issue (10-11), the death of James (12), confronting pagan forces (13-14), and the council at Jerusalem (15). Yet, instead of tearing the church apart, these problems developed greater unity. The church became more spiritually powerful than ever, and souls were added daily to the church.

Amazingly, there is no mention of the Great Commission in the book of Acts. Yet, that is exactly what happened. Acts describes the church, empowered by the Holy Spirit, growing without hindrance to touch the ends of the earth. Truly, in Christ, every obstacle becomes an opportunity!

EPHESIANS 4
THE CHURCH IS A SCHOOL OF THE SPIRIT

In Ephesians 4 we discover that the church is a school of the Spirit. Here we learn to minister to one another, to disciple one another, and to equip one another to serve God! In my book, *Spiritual Gifts: a Fresh Look*, I point out that Romans 12, 1 Corinthians 12-13 and Ephesians 4 are written from the same outline! There are over twenty five key similarities in all three passages! Paul's key instructions on spiritual gifts, written to three of the strongest churches of the first century, were structured on the same basic outline!

Paul uses school terminology. In this chapter Paul talks about knowing Christ (4:20), being taught in him (4:21-22), to have new attitudes (4:23), to speak truthfully (4:25) to control emotions (4:26), to build up others according to their needs (4:29).

Jesus is the master teacher, the curriculum, and the administrator of this school! When we graduate we shall become more like Jesus! We learn how to minister to one another. We become disciples living a lifestyle in the Spirit. In church we learn, and then we go out to serve. (For a more complete discussion of the church as a school in Ephesians 4, see Marcus Barth, *Ephesians 4-6, Vol 34A*, Garden City, N.Y.: Doubleday and Company, Inc., 1974, pp. 529-533).

I have learned so much from others in the body of Christ. Confucius said it well, "Where three people walk together, one of them is my teacher." Years ago I met a young man while I was teaching in Western Pentecostal Bible College in Canada. He was a fairly new Christian, and newly married. He came to our school unsure of himself. His marriage was going through major struggles. He did not feel God could use him.

He came into my office for counseling. I asked him what he would like to do. He said he wished that he could start a Christian counseling center in conjunction with a local church. I encouraged him. I told him he was one of the sharpest students we ever had at the college. I told him I was convinced that God would use him mightily.

He queried, "Do you really think so? Do you really believe God could use me?" I assured him I did and I referred him to Dr. Richard Dobbins, who headed a major counseling ministry called EMERGE, and who taught counseling at the graduate level. Paul obtained his Master's Degree with that program and ultimately started the largest Christian counseling ministry affiliated with a local church in North America. He had authored three books on counseling. God had richly blessed his ministry.

After many years our paths crossed again in Sacramento, California. We were attending a district council convention of pastors of Northern California and Nevada. I saw him walking up the aisle after a session and he saw me. We met in the foyer and hugged each other like long-lost friends.

He said to me, "Dr. Lim, out of all the people in the world I prayed would be here today, it was you and my pastor from New Jersey! You see, I am being ordained tonight, and I so wanted you here!"

I rejoiced with him for attaining this great milestone in his ministry, but I asked him why he prayed I would be here at his ordination. He replied, "Because it was your words that spoke life into me and gave me confidence to move to the future. My life was changed by your impartation to me as a young Christian going to Bible college!"

I said, "Paul, I'm so grateful that I was able to be such a blessing to you at one point in your life. At that point I was strong and you were weak. But, truthfully, I have just been through a terrible experience in my ministry. Paul, you are my friend and a professional counselor, can you help me to walk through this dark season of my life?" He said, "Of course, Dr. Lim. Come to my home and we'll talk and pray together." He literally walked me through my trial to a new perspective in what Christ wanted to do in my life. But the story does not end there.

A few years later, he called me in Singapore. "Dr. Lim, I am going to a conference in the Philippines and it would make my trip complete if I could come and minister at your church." I replied, "Of course, Paul, you'll be a great blessing to Grace Assembly."

We had a wonderful weekend of meetings. I drove him out to the airport and we sat in the cafeteria sharing our thoughts as we waited for his flight. Then he opened up and said, "Dr. Lim, I do not understand what is going on within me. I have started and developed the largest Christian counseling service in North America connected to a local church. I have written books on counseling. I teach a large adult Bible class in church. Yet I feel deeply frustrated. I feel there is more."

I paused for a moment and said, "Perhaps God is calling you to be a senior pastor." He looked at me and said, "Do you really think that God could use me as a senior pastor?" I replied, "You will make an outstanding one." I heard from him a few weeks later. He told me that he wept on the flight back to San Francisco. Not only did he know God had called him to be a pastor, but he knew which church he was to pastor! The only problem was his friend was already the pastor of that church!

Amazingly, a few days later the friend called him to say he was resigning from that church and, would Paul consider being the senior pastor? God has mightily used Pastor Paul Goulet in the International Church of Las Vegas (ICLV). It has exploded in growth from about 200 people to over 4000 regular attendees. God's mighty hand has been upon his life and ministry! His wife, Denise, who was formerly shy and withdrawn, has become a great, dynamic preacher as well.

Over the last several years Paul has continued to impart into my life, and I into his. That is the nature of the church. Sometimes one is strong and the other is weak. At another time one is weak and the other is strong. We learn together, grow together, weep together, and rejoice together. The church is a school. In this school we learn to minister gifts and glorify God! We learn to defeat the devil!

EPHESIANS 5: 6:9
LIFE IS MISSION

We are made for a purpose. In Ephesians 5 and 6 the Apostle Paul teaches on husband-wife relationships, parent-child relationships, and masters and slaves (perhaps in contemporary terms "the employer-employee relationship"). All of these relationships are part and parcel of our mission. In the drama of redemption, each of these relationships is to picture our relationship to Christ. We are to show His love. We are to submit to the Father's plan. We are to glorify God in every act. He is our leader. To Him we freely submit our gifts, talents and energies.

By obeying our Master we declare God's way is the best way. By reflecting our Master's sacrificial love in practical ways to others we are declaring Christ's love for the church to angels, demons, and pre-believers.

We proclaim the gospel by our lives. All of our relationships are governed by our relationship to God. In this way we declare that God has won and Satan has lost. We affect the cosmos by all of our actions. We fill the universe with the glory of God. This has been covered in greater detail in the first section of this book.

It has been said, "Paul's theology was grace, and his ethics was gratitude." For Paul, everything was the grace of God. Salvation, his calling to ministry, the gifts of the Spirit, the body of Christ, suffering and life itself was the grace of God.

We deserve nothing. Our only response to God's marvelous grace must be gratitude. We do not serve God because we are forced to, or to earn God's favor, or because we have no trials. We serve God simply because we are so grateful for everything God has done for us. No matter what the circumstances, nor how people treat us, we will faithfully serve Him because He pours out His abundant grace upon us. Each member of the body of Christ is God's gift to us. We must learn to appreciate each other and impart God's unconditional love to each other. Our whole life purpose is a mission to declare God's glory.

It is important to see the overall structure of Ephesians. Ephesians 1-3 is worship. Ephesians 4:1-6:9 is walk. Ephesians 6:10-20 is warfare. Note the following diagram:

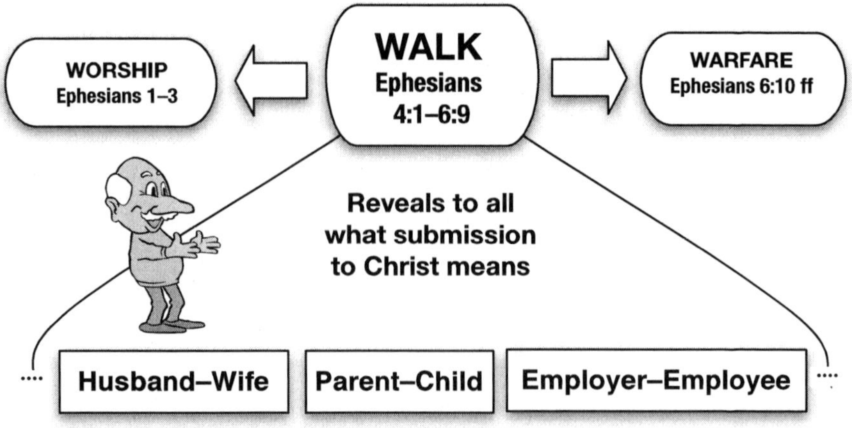

1. Worship precedes walk and walk precedes warfare. Effective walk in Christ is built upon a life of worship.

2. Strong worship and walk are necessary for effective warfare. We cannot defeat the devil if we are not worshipping God and living consistent Christian lives.

3. For Paul our walk is our worship. We do not just verbally praise God. We live out our praise to God as a living worship.

4. For Paul, our walk is our warfare. I do not defeat the devil simply by fasting and prayer and binding the enemy. I defeat the devil by loving my wife, by being a godly father, and by treating my fellow believers in a Christ like manner.

   If I do things God's way I will ultimately win against Satan. Every act I perform in this drama is a prophetic act declaring God's victory and Satan's defeat. I live out my mission through my whole life.

5. Our walk reveals to angels and demons and pre-believers our submission to Christ. The church submits to Jesus because

He has already won the victory over Satan, sin, and death. We know, because He has won, we too shall win! Our submission proclaims the good news in Jesus!

EPHESIANS 6:10-20

WARFARE

Ephesians 6:10-20 speak of our warfare against the devil. It is the ultimate point of this epistle. We shall win against Satan! Let us notice several key things about the armor of God.

First, every verb is plural. The armor of God is for all the people of God collectively. We have previously taught that the armor of God was something each of us must put on individually. But none of us can win this war on our own. The Christian life is not about superstars. We need the rest of the army!

The Roman legion was the strongest army of its day. They learned to march together. The front row held their shields in front of them. The second row of troops held their shields high above them. When the Roman soldiers marched, they looked like an invincible tank moving relentlessly to victory. When we learn to march in unity, protecting one another and fighting the warfare together, we shall have incredible victory.

A famous Chinese story tells of a dying father who had ten sons who were always fighting and bickering amongst themselves. He wanted to teach them a lesson before he died. He gathered all his sons around his bedside.

He gave each of them a single stick. He challenged his sons to break the stick. Each of the sons easily broke his stick. Then, from underneath the bed, the father took a bundle of ten sticks tied together. He challenged them to break the ten sticks. None of them could break the ten sticks bundled together.

The wise father then said to his sons, "If you go out to face the world individually, the world will break you apart, just as you broke the individual sticks. But if you face the world united, nothing can break you!" Even so, if the Christian army can learn to march forward together, we will be an army that will chase every demon away. We will win victory after victory!

Second, we see the Messiah putting on similar armor. Isaiah 11:5 says of the Messiah, "Righteousness will be his belt and faithfulness the sash around his waist." Isaiah 59:17 says "He put on righteousness as his breastplate, and the helmet of salvation on his head; he put on the garments of vengeance and wrapped himself in zeal as in a cloak."

Revelation 19:11-16 says concerning the Messiah, the rider on the white horse "...With justice he judges and makes war...He is dressed in a robe dipped in blood and his name is the Word of God... Out of His mouth comes a sharp sword with which to strike down the nations." Great victory takes place as the Messiah dons His armor and fulfills His mission!

Third, many scholars tell us that the armor Paul describes is really Jesus Himself. When Paul tells us to put on the new man and to put off the old man he is saying put on Jesus Christ. Who is the belt of truth? Jesus said "I am the way the truth, and the life" (John 14:6).Who is the breastplate of righteousness? Indeed Jesus is our righteousness. Who is the helmet of salvation? Jesus is our salvation.

When we cover our minds with His salvation and set our minds on the things above, we protect our mind from satanic attack. Who is the shield of faith? Our faith is built totally upon Jesus Christ. Who is the gospel of peace that becomes our shoes? Jesus is our peace who has broken down every wall between us and God. Who is the sword of the Spirit, the word of God? Jesus is the living Word of God and when we declare His powerful words, the demons flee. By putting on the armor we can stand firm against the devil. God then fights our battles for us. His victory becomes ours.

The themes of the drama of redemption are found in this overview of Ephesians. Give God all the glory. From Genesis to Revelation this is the key theme. Overcome every hurdle. No obstacle is too big because Christ has broken down every wall. Learn together in the school of the Spirit. Disciple one another, edify one another, speak the truth in love. These are tools to empower one another. Life is mission. Live out your life on the platform of the drama of redemption. Every act is a prophetic act. Win the warfare by putting on the armor of Christ.

This is living life on the highest level. When we see our role in this great cosmic drama of redemption we are lifted to our highest calling. As we act out our part, we show God's wisdom to angels and demons and pre-believers. When we face life God's way, God wins and Satan loses! When God wins–we win—big!